WING STROKE

BOOK TWO OF THE WINGS SERIES

WING STROKE

m.a. ARANA

atmosphere press

For all who have supported the expansion of this series.
As always, for my dear sister, Maria Elena.
May your soul rest in peace.

CHARACTERS

AVANS

Avan Kingdom - pronounced 'Ay - von,' means to 'preserve and protect' in India; the kingdom is made up of winged people sworn to protect the earth; a group of Avans is called a flock; Avans sprout wings at ten years old

Mabon Sevilla - pronounced 'May - bun Se - vee - yah,' is the first half breed and prince of Ava; his name means 'Divine Son' in Welsh; has Heterochromia iridium (two different-colored eyes); trained and studied to become King of Ava

Sada - pronounced 'Say - duh,' Mabon's daughter is considered full Avan due to her mother being Avan; the name means 'Pure One' in Japanese; also has Heterochromia iridium; inherits new powers

Twins - Xander - pronounced 'Zan - dur' (means 'Defender of the People' in Greek) and Xio - pronounced 'Zee - o' (means Ready for 'Battle' in Spanish); twins are nine going on ten years of age, ready to sprout their Avan wings; training their magic and fighting skills

Romeo - pronounced 'Roe - mee - o,' Mabon's Belgian Shepherd dog on Earth is a loyal companion; the name means 'From Rome' in Italian

Queen Kalani - pronounced 'Ka - la - nee,' the name means 'The Heavens' in Polynesian/Hawaiian; she is the true queen of the Avans; she fell in love with a human man; her wings are the largest of the flock; ready to pass on the throne to her son, Mabon

Willa – pronounced 'We – la'; the queen's new attendant; name means feminine form of 'Will,' origin is American

Galeno – pronounced 'Guh – lee – no,' the head of the royal army and Mabon's ex-mentor; Ibis is his niece; name means 'Calm' and is a form of Galen-Spanish

Oda – pronounced 'Oh – da,' the name means 'Great Field' in Japanese and medieval Irish of unknown meaning; he provides counsel to the royals; he is the oldest Avan and the strongest in terms of magic, but has limitations when it comes to the future; has taken Sada as his pupil

Ibis – pronounced 'Ee – bis,' she was Galeno's niece, became a Garghon queen; the name means 'Long-legged Bird'; she was Mabon's mate who died (and no longer has wings), and now is plotting her return to the living to take the throne and rob the life essence of Avans to become immortal

Edouard – pronounced 'Ed – word,' is Ava's flying instructor; he is Mabon's best friend from childhood; the name means 'Wealthy Guardian'; training further to be a better warrior

Camille – pronounced 'Cam – eel,' is Galeno's mate, magic teacher, and strongest Avan sorceress; the name means 'Perfect' in French; her daughter is Urmi

Quoba – pronounced 'Kwoh – bah,' is an elite Avan warrior known for his strength; he has recently been promoted to second in command of the Avan defense force; the name means 'Good' and the origin is Aboriginal

Urmi – pronounced 'Oor – me'; daughter of Galeno and Camille; she is four years old and befriends the twins; her name means 'Wave,' origin is Indian (Sanskrit)

Declan – pronounced 'Dee – klan'; name means 'Full of Goodness' of Irish origin; he is knowledgeable about herbs and healing bodies; also trained to fight

Fate – pronounced 'Fay – t'; responsible for choosing mates

Humans

Gerardo Sevilla – pronounced 'Heh – rar – doe,' Mabon's Latino father was a farmer who died mysteriously when Mabon was about 15; the name means 'Spear Brave' in Spanish; he wed Queen Kalani during her stay on Earth; his duel-colored eyes were passed on to descendants through Kalani's Avan blood

Tori – pronounced 'Toh – ree,' is Mabon's human wife; mother to twin boys, Xander and Xio; the name means 'Winner' or 'Conqueror' in English

Gabriel Rosales – pronounced 'Gaib – rl Roe – sa – less,' used to be a field worker for the Sevillas; the name means 'God is my Strength'; the secret keeper for Mabon about the Avans; is in love with Sada; training to be a warrior; has a brother in the Air Force named Jaime

Mr. and Mrs. Rosales – Gabriel's parents who were killed by the Garghons

Jaime Rosales – pronounced 'Hi – meh'; Gabriel's brother; name means 'Supplanter,' origin is Spanish [Supplanter often refers to governments and rulers of countries]; after learning of his parents' deaths, he seeks answers to what killed them from a secretive brother; overcome with grief and anger, he is taken by the Garghons

GARGHONS

Garghons – pronounced 'Gar – guns,' are a force unknown to humans; half beast–half man with leathery wings that have no feathers like a gargoyle's; large yellow eyes; they hiss and cry out in bird-like manner (caw); can make talon-like fingers; usually smell of burned flesh

Nafuna – pronounced 'Nah – foo – na,' was the head Garghon sentinel; the name means 'Delivered Feet First' of African origin; good combatant; died in the arena battling Sada

Waqar – pronounced 'Way – car,' is the Garghon King; the name means 'Majesty and Dignity' in Arabic; has large curved horns on his head; he wants to use Avan's souls to power his own; can summon portals with his breath; he discovers a lost spell that causes environmental catastrophes on Earth; considers Xio his property

Tamesis – pronounced 'Ta – meh – ses'; Garghon warrior witch whose magic is almost as strong as the Garghon King; name means 'Dark One,' English origin

Baqir – pronounced 'Becker'; new head Garghon sentinel; name means 'To Rip Open,' origin is Arabic; name of the river Thames

Aja – pronounced 'Ay – ja'; the beast who protects the dark magic book the Garghons found; name means 'to drive, propel' of Indian origin; the beast brings forth desire from its male victims

CHAPTER

1

light echoed past the horizon
the backdrop of soldiers through valley and bark
a bird's heartless chirp
each note dripping at your feet
the price for mending darkness
covered with the years I heard my mother crying...

A sword in between wings marked the tall firestone doors to the Avan castle's recreation area. Sentries remained stationary on either side with glowing shields and armor. Two four-foot speckled falcon statues adorned the walls. Through the gates was a double, clear water-glass door where the crystal pool rippled from the body floating on it. The water massaged Mabon's skin, stroking his aching muscles from the recent Garghon encounter on the uninhabited island of Tetepare, one that ended as briefly as it began. With arms outstretched, he let the water's motion soothe his piling responsibilities. Responsibilities an Avan prince could no longer avoid, including raising his half-Avan sons. Once he opened his eyes, the high, angular glass ceiling let in the sun. He turned over and swam to the edge. The rays warmed his shoulders like oil rubbed down.

Stepping out of the pool, Mabon reached for the towel

hanging on a tree limb and patted his face dry. The yellow flowers burst open, filling the large space with their fragrance. As forthcoming king, he had the whole makeshift room to himself, and his thoughts meandered from the last four years on Ava. The Garghons had stolen his family to facilitate Ibis taking the throne, and he would do anything to prevent it from happening again.

His mother, the queen, hadn't completely healed from the poison Ibis had given her those years ago. Each day, she aged, which was unusual for an Avan, and made it hard to accept, especially as gray hair grew at her temples. The permanent reminder that his probationary period was almost over had her going over the rites repeatedly. Mabon slapped the towel on his lap and squeezed the corner of it. The inevitability of being king once she lets go of her spark. It was a task he never wanted to be part of, but obligation and responsibility had superseded any wants. He was Avan. And when the sun sets, wise Oda suggested his mother officially announce her retirement. Though the Avans had finally accepted him as their own, it was too soon to tell whether his children would have enough Avan blood to be kings since Sada had no inclination to lead with a crown. Mabon sighed and patted his hair dry, wincing at the soreness of his shoulder.

"I prefer you without the added clothing."

Lowering the towel, Mabon spotted his wife, Tori, by the entrance to the chamber, past four trees and their long branches. He smiled and wrapped the towel around his waist.

"I prefer it the other way," he said.

Tori leaned on the entrance and watched her husband approach her. His animal gait intoxicated her, as that first night they made love. He wanted to wait until they got married, and it was worth it. Still, her skin heated the closer he got, and she caressed her forearm in anticipation.

Taking her hand in his, Mabon pulled Tori toward him. He brushed his cheek on hers and greeted her with a kiss, which she returned with the same ardent passion, parting her lips. He kissed her neck.

She let out a moan, and a few seconds later, backed away.

Still holding her hand, Mabon asked, "What is it?"

"Can we talk first?" She tilted her head to one side. Her shoulder-length hair followed.

He held her cheek with his free hand and nodded.

"Don't you think it's time to let the boys visit Earth more often?"

"They go every weekend." He brushed her soft hair behind her ear, inhaling the fresh scent of peaches she loved.

"I know." Tori kissed his hand and led him toward the pool. Her bare feet felt the coolness cover them as she stepped in. "Maybe we could work something out. I feel they're missing the normalcy of being human."

"If you don't think talking back to their tutors isn't human enough, I wonder what is," Mabon said, chuckling.

"You know what I mean." She squeezed his hand, pulling it toward her.

"I do, but they are expected to behave above all since they are of royal blood."

"They haven't exactly been able to blend in with kids their age."

"What happened to them has left a deep scar." He stepped down to be at eye level with her and put her head on his shoulder. "Xander still recalls the details of the Rosales' deaths. Xio can still see Ibis' vacant eyes in nightmares."

"That's what I mean," she said, moving her head away. "They need to spend time away from this."

He wiggled his nose with hers. "I understand, but they're at an age when they'll sprout their wings."

"So, I'm too late?" She puckered. "After five days, I'd have to settle for birthdays every other year."

He hugged her and caressed her hair. "Maybe we can add another day for a while before their next growth spurt."

"You talk about them as if they weren't children." She pulled away and softly slapped his shoulder. The light from above lit the tops of the ripples in the water like fireflies floating away from her.

"Tori, I'm just preparing you for what's to come." And he was sure the Garghons were only toying with them, planning, and preying on them until they got their talons on the twins.

"I'm sorry, I just don't like my children being referred to as prey."

"Prey?"

"Okay, maybe not prey."

"Can we talk about this later?" he asked, kissing her hand.

Her big brown eyes met his, and she wanted to savor every moment she got with him. Smiling, she pulled him closer to her, removing his towel. "How about another dip?"

Landing on the uncharted island with a dormant volcano, Baqir's feet picked up dust and pebbles before they settled a few feet from them. He closed his wings and slipped through the enlarged plants in front of the cave entrance. The cold forced itself on his dark skin, and he shivered, then proceeded further into the damp darkness. He used his talon to scratch the rocky surface, leaving a line etched onto it as part of the texture. The friction caused a few sparks, and he half smiled.

"What news have you brought?" A voice boomed from the lit entrance at the end of the tunnel.

Once at the entrance, Baqir groaned and bent on one knee. "Master."

"Well?" King Waqar tapped his talons on the arm of his throne.

Patience had grown weary in the king's heart since he had explained the Garghon origins years before and the reason they could not procreate. Born from death, they live with death; thus, they must conquer others as the law dictates for their kind.

Lifting his chin, Baqir said, "Ava continues to scout its perimeter."

"And the children?" Waqar turned away and watched a set of small critters he had collected crawl inside a glass box. Their scorpion tails were out of sync with their abdomens.

"They are doing extremely well." He licked his lip. "They visit Earth more often than we counted on."

"Get me someone on the inside before they suspect."

"After four years, they must have forgotten."

Waqar pounded his fist on the arm of the chair, denting it. His fiery yellow eyes whirled, and he blew out smoke from his nostrils. "Forgotten isn't a word for Ava. Nothing is forgotten."

Baqir cringed back from the smoke, and said, "Forgive me, mighty one." He placed his hand over his chest.

"Rest assured that the boy will be ours." Waqar curled his talons. "Nafuna and the others did not die a warrior's death merely to be forgotten."

"Yes, my lord." Baqir bowed his horned head. "We will not let the Avans shortchange us again. You have my word."

The Garghon king leaned forward. Larger than the rest of his warriors, his shadow covered Baqir's body, and the Garghon gulped.

"So be it," he said.

CHAPTER

2

Knocking down his third opponent, Gabriel turned and eyed Sada from behind the gate in the arena. He removed the Avan helmet forged for him by Quoba and wiped the sweat off his chin. Saluting the downed Avan, he turned and walked to her.

"How was that?"

"Not bad." She grinned. Her white wings were bent at her sides.

"Not bad?" He pulled his head back in surprise. "I sweat like a pig, and that's all you say?"

Sada closed the gap between them and grabbed his helmet, placing it back on. "You're fighting students. It's time you fight true warriors."

"Maybe I've earned the title by now." He scrunched up his nose, like Sada had done many times, and touched the tip of hers.

She slammed his shoulder with her staff. "Come."

Gabriel backed up, inhaled, and took up his fighting stance. She swayed the staff to the left, then up and across. He blocked it with his shield and went for his sword.

Sada raised her arm to distract him and managed to slide the staff under his feet, sending him flat on the ground and picking up dirt. His helmet pushed his neck up, cranking it like a broken handle.

Swiftly, Sada jumped on him, her hair in a ponytail falling forward, her white wings outstretched, and she pressed the end of her staff right below his Adam's apple.

Some Avan students watched in awe as she pressed the staff's end a little more.

"I surrender." Gabriel coughed and raised his hands in defeat.

The Avans stopped their exercises and clapped. One managed to yell that it was about time. The sound bounced off the expansive dome area.

Sada's eyes shone like the sea, amused at his fall. Her hair was adorned with a leaf clip he gave her last year.

"Can I get up now?" Gabriel tried to avoid swallowing. He savored her touch at this distance. It excited parts of his body he wasn't allowed to, as long as they weren't official mates.

She removed her staff, made her wings disappear, and helped him up. "There is still much for you to learn."

"I don't mind you teaching me." He leaned close to her and reached for her waist. His fingers barely touched her when she shook her head and stepped back.

"It's time you had another mentor," she said, her voice trailing.

"Why? I learn good with you."

"It's 'well.' Remember the lessons?"

He waved his tan arms, then brought them to his side. "Galeno *es muy amenazante...* intimidating."

But Sada had moved away and almost made it out the gate before he caught on to her arm. She pulled, then stopped.

"What is it?" He frowned and bore his eyes into hers. Worry seeped into Gabriel's brown eyes, and lines formed on his forehead.

She placed her hand on his flustered cheek.

Years ago, they pledged a love so great that it made her knees tremble each time she saw him, but now, all she could think about was how she was going to lose him. She was a princess, and there would always be danger from being too close. Tori knew all about that. She almost lost her family.

"*Señor* Sevilla married an Avan, and your father married a human." He let go of her arm. "They made me secret keeper."

She massaged the area he had touched. "I'm not my father, Gabriel."

Stunned, he took off his helmet and wiped the sweat trickling down his forehead from the exercises. Could she be that strong and bring a flock of her own?

"I don't care what everyone thinks, either."

"It's not that." She viewed the guards behind her. Each at their station. Their stance was practiced, their gaze fixed on the outside, and every inch of Avan blood. "They talk because they can."

Forming fists, he looked away, taking in the arena they had left through a twelve-foot-wide entrance. Avans, who had every right to be there practicing their skills and honing them for what their role will be in life. They continued the day's routine. He was a farmer, a fieldhand with ambitions to make his own staples. He made things grow. He lowered his eyes and viewed the calluses on his hands from holding the sword. Training harder than the year before to stay ahead of the group, to change his role from the outdated secret keeper, and to please his warrior girlfriend, who was as adept at handling a weapon as she was at thinking a spell.

Again, Sada cupped her hand under his cheek. The tips of her fingers ran along his growing whiskers.

He turned to her with glazed eyes.

"I don't want to hurt you, Gabriel."

"What do you call this?"

She removed her hand, leaving behind a warmth that filled Gabriel's heart.

"I need time to think."

"Why? It's been four years, Sada," he said with exasperation. "*¿Cuanto más tiempo necesitas para saber si me quieres* *lo suficiente para estar conmigo?"*

When he said those sharp words, it hurt Sada. Gulping, she crossed her arms. "I haven't learned enough Spanish to know what you mean."

Letting the helmet fall and roll off to the side, he said, "Read my mind, Sada." He got hold of her hands and brought her arms down. *"Te quiero mucho.* I want to be an Avan just to kiss your tired feet." He held her shoulders and smoothed his hands on her forearms, settling on her fingers. "I love you so much, I can't think of anything but you." He caressed her fingers with his, then said, "And I wish you loved me as much, too."

Sada felt a lump the size of a kiwi form in her throat. "I can't..." She shook her hands free from his grasp. Tears forming, she ran out into the hall.

Gabriel watched the woman he loved escape from him like sand through a beaker. Picking up his helmet from the floor, he glanced at the Avans guarding the doors to the arena and noticed the slits in their eyes.

The scent of molasses mixed with gasoline filled the cave as a dozen Garghons formed a circle around a found object. It was taken from the island they had battled with Avans the day before. They were hunched over as green hues hit their faces. One used her yellowed teeth to break open the lock, and another used his claws to peer into the large book. A gust of wind blew the first pages off the spine, causing the Garghons to drop the object on the ground and run after them before returning to the circle where the Garghon witch flew down. Their shadows silhouetted on the rock wall; two feet higher from the fire's light.

"With this, King Waqar would have no trouble bringing Ava to its knees," Tamesis said. She coiled her sharp talons around the dropped book.

The Garghons threw their weapons up and made grunting noises.

"Ibis must be proud to have shared such knowledge." She raised the book high and turned with a snicker. The brightness from it pierced the sky with an invisible force that could be seen through an opening above.

The group pounded their weapons on the rock walls, and along with their shrieking, they caused rock pebbles to fall from above on the sandy ground. They danced around the circle as Tamesis recalled the loose pages and placed them back inside. She turned the pages in the book, landing on a particular page that glowed, causing her teeth to lengthen from the light.

CHAPTER
3

The room next to the queen's study had been in disuse since Mabon's exile but had now been occupied by the twins for learning and relaxing. It was large and contained all the tools, papers, and necessary books. Xander's mother would sometimes join them and help with their instruction, as would all the tutors who gave them a homeschooled education. Cutting the last piece of fiberboard needed to complete the castle, Xander placed it on the top of the tower with care. The castle was a reconstruction of the pyramid-like one on Ava for his homework assignment in architecture, but with an added wing to the back of the stables. Stepping back to get a better look, he bumped into his twin, Xio, who worked on the ground.

"Hey!"

"Oops." Xander tried moving away from the workspace Xio claimed below him, and accidentally collided with the wall put up with tree sap. "Really, oops."

With a scowl that would break rock, Xio rose and knocked down his brother's castle. In a flutter, the pieces fell off the table like hail.

Romeo yelped as he awakened from a short nap. *"What's going on?"* he projected.

"Nothing," Xio vented through their mind link.

Xander sighed, collecting all the pieces and getting some

stuck to his palm. "He knocked down my homework again."

Realizing Xio didn't mean to vent the way he did, Romeo nuzzled the boy's thigh.

"I'm not the one with hippo feet." Xio crossed his arms.

Romeo nudged him again.

"Fine." He lifted his arms and started helping his brother.

Lifting the glass used for the windows, Xander said, "I can build it again. No problem."

With throat dry and sniffing the wooden chips, Xio looked at his twin with furrowed eyebrows. "You mean, you won't tell mom."

"It's 'mother,' Xio."

"Mom likes it." Xio shrugged. "The other way sounds too... too..."

"Avan?"

The twins turned in the direction of the voice, where Willa, the queen's new attendant stood. Tall and athletically built, her dark robes cradled her shoulders, stretching over her entire body. Due to the length of the robe, her feet stepped on the fabric when she walked. It used to make them laugh.

Romeo wagged his tail, greeted her with a slight hop, and said to the boys, *"Offer your greetings and apology."*

Xio moved his mouth to the side and clumped all the pieces of his building together.

"We're sorry if we caused so much noise," Xander finally said. "We hope the queen didn't wake because of us."

Willa smiled. Her lips moistened with pink to match her cheeks. "It's been a long time since the queen would let the scruples of children bother her peace." She moved toward them, the robe covered her neck and she looked like a crane bird. She bent on one knee, her chestnut hair fell on her shoulders, smelling of roses in full bloom, and she picked up a piece from behind them, handing it to Xio.

He gulped and took it. "Sorry."

Rising, she brushed her wavy hair back. "Queen Kalani

wants to speak to you both."

Woof! Romeo barked.

Nodding, Willa continued, "Make sure they get cleaned up, Romeo."

Woof!

"Good. It has been a long time since anyone presented themselves in such dire states as this." Her grin softened her face, and she turned to leave the workroom.

After the twins prepared for their meeting, Romeo led them toward the hall. Though the twins have roamed the halls at different hours, each time seemed to be a first. The high ceiling, the crystal swan chandeliers, the slanted windows cut into sizeable polygons, and the ornate doors that welcomed every member of Ava were artistic feats. Guards stood at the entrance wherever a royal was and in front of important rooms.

Once they were ten feet from the queen's study, Romeo departed, leaving them in the care of the guards ahead.

Soon, Xio took Xander's arm and asked, "What do you think she wants to talk about?"

"Maybe she wants to see how we're doing."

"Come on, Xander, what if it's about my headaches?"

Xander paused and glanced up at the ceiling, observing the shadows made by the light. Lately, he has been noticing things in more detail than before. Maybe that's why he watches the way Willa's clothes fit her curves.

"I don't think so," he finally replied.

"Okay, what about you being able to use mom's locket? Even if the power is hidden away in some vault?" He let go of Xander's arm. "She's super powerful, you know?"

Xander shook his head. "Don't you think I'd know it?" He lowered his eyes and continued walking. "Now, stop worrying. The queen's our grandmother after all."

Scratching his forehead, Xio adjusted his shirt and followed his brother to the queen's room. His heart beat at a fast rate, as if it bumped against his chest trying to get out. He placed his hand over it in an attempt to stop it, but it only got worse.

"You ready?" Xander placed his hand over his brother's.

"Huh? Yeah."

"It's 'yes,' Xio."

He nodded and widened his dark eyes. "Okay, okay, yes."

They stood in front of the guards, who wore a shiny helmet where the helm meets the faceplate, protecting their noses, and allowing their eyes to see.

Without an introduction, the guards tapped their staffs on the ground, and the doors opened. The twins moved in, bent on one knee, and placed their fists over their chests.

"Come forward, children of Mabon," Queen Kalani said from her seated position. The wooden back of the chair had peacocks carved onto it, similar to the ones on her chamber doors. She sat beside an ornate desk filled with loose papers and glass bottles. She wore a soft yellow dress with pearls fastened at the hem.

The twins rose and approached the queen. The doors closed behind them, causing air to rush past them.

Willa stepped out from a revolving door, bringing other bottles into the study room. She smiled at them and set the items down. "Is there anything more, my queen?"

"No, thank you, my dear." The queen waved her hand, and the long sleeves followed her arm like aerial silk. "You may return in a short while."

Willa curtsied and bowed her head, then walked backwards toward the door she entered from.

Queen Kalani turned to her grandchildren, her deep blue eyes were like the sea: calm, inviting, and mysterious.

"You wonder why you've come?"

They gulped.

"Like your father, I must ask that you accept the fate of leading this kingdom."

"But we are too young." Xander knew he spoke out of turn and bit his lip before saying, "Being part Avan doesn't give us the right to rule."

The queen spread her long fingers on the table top, smoothing out the threads on the mat placed there. "You sound like your father, and I am glad, for a king must never feel superior to those he leads."

"Is this a test?" Xio asked, scrunching his face.

Queen Kalani's eyes softened as she raised her chin. "Consider it the beginning of the end." She stood, took each of their hands, and guided them toward the angular window.

Outside, the wind blew against the green trees, pulling leaves down and up like a wave. Xander watched the clouds behind them zoom past like an Arctic storm. The scent of wet cement and moss filled him with anticipation for the moon.

"Both of you are special," Queen Kalani said. "Sada has many gifts, too, and unlike the two of you, she has made a choice."

Xio pulled away and asked, "Is Sada leaving us?"

The queen looked down and shook her head. "So young to have worry lines..." Her earrings swayed like the treetops outside. "She has become a master pupil in the arts and will join Oda to finalize Camille's tutelage."

"She's gonna become a witch?" Xio gasped.

Xander slapped his forehead. "Sorceress."

"Your sister has chosen to support the future rulers with her talents." She took Xio's shoulders under her grasp and blinked repeatedly. "What is this 'gonna' you uttered?"

"Oh," Xio rubbed the back of his head, "I mean 'going to' your highness."

"A king must know how to speak, Xio. You will soon grow your wings and learn to harness the energy within you and not let it control you." She let go of him and touched her chest, catching her breath. "I have faith you will wisely choose your destiny."

Xio tilted his head to the right. *Did his grandmother want them to follow their father?*

What about the Garghons? They didn't want him to take the throne. Did they?

"Are you feeling well, your majesty?" Xander took her hand in his after he caught Xio's thoughts. A short sensation ran from his toes that lit up the veins on his arm to the rest of his side, making the hairs stand on end. Once it radiated back to his hand, the pulsing pressure made him squint and feel faint. He wasn't sure whether the queen had given him something magical or if it was a clash of their powers.

Queen Kalani wiped the boy's forehead. "So young to have worry lines..." She waved her hand. "Leave me, and remember your place, sons of Mabon, for the beginning will soon be the end."

CHAPTER

4

Oda removed his glasses and squeezed the bridge of his nose. A slight tension traveled to the side of his head, landing at a random spot in the back of his head.

"Are you well, wise one?" Sada set down the recent conjuring manuscript Oda had for her to study. She reached for his free hand. It trembled under her touch.

Oda gestured a response, saying he was fine, but Sada could tell by the paleness of his skin and the lost look in his clear eyes that he wasn't. She frowned and summoned Camille telepathically.

"I know you call her, but I assure you, I'm all right." Oda placed his glasses back on and closed his book. The faint odor of dust blew past Sada's nose, followed by a whiff of vanilla brewing in the cauldron to their left. "Have you looked at the spell? It's an ancient one not used often."

"Master, you're not well. Why don't you let Camille and I treat you?"

"Child," he touched her cheek and met her bi-colored eyes, "Your healing cannot save me from fate."

Her eyes moistened. Oda had mentioned his spirit was prepared to leave him, but not like this. She had just started learning from him after her father approved. There was still so much he could teach. Viewing the walls covered from floor to ceiling with odd bottles and jars, Sada stopped at the table layered with scrolls and a number of texts. Ancient works she hoped to satiate her mind with.

The doors opened as Camille waved to them. She wore a dark forest gothic dress with long sleeves. Her black hair had violet highlights that matched her plump lips. Urmi, her daughter, who was as lovely as her parents, followed behind. She greeted the eldest member of the flock and turned to Sada, whose own face paled in comparison.

"Please leave us, Princess." Camille gave Urmi's hand to her. "Take her to the garden for a while."

"But—" Sada stopped herself from asking the reason. Camille knew Oda would talk to her in private about things he wouldn't tell his pupil. So Sada bowed and walked beside Urmi. Not until they reached the door and closed it, did she hear them speak.

"Eavesdropping is a no-no," Urmi said, as black strands of hair fell over her big green eyes. They watched Sada lean next to the door, her head tilting left to right like an owl.

Kneeling in front of Urmi, Sada said, "You're right, little one. I apologize."

Urmi's face lit up, bringing her chiseled nose to light. It resembled her father's, and she used it well at four and a half years of age.

When her father first arrived on Ava, Galeno struck the prince for being a half-breed; now, he protects the kingdom so the twins do not have to share the same fate. So far, the Avans are pleased with Prince Mabon's rule.

"Come, let's find Romeo." Sada stood.

"You're worried."

Sada closed her eyes briefly. "Yes, I'm worried my teacher will soon come to pass and join the four winds."

"You can't help that." Urmi picked up her black fairy dress skirt with purple trimmings and skipped ahead of her. She stopped at the end of the pathway to Oda's cottage. "Mother will have a plan. She always does."

Crossing her arms, Sada sighed. "Little Camille knows something. Would you care to let us plain Avans have a hint?"

Urmi gestured for the princess to come closer. When she did, Urmi took her hand. "Some of us can't live forever."

Sada pulled her hand away. "I've felt death, little one, but this is the Avan whose knowledge of past kings and queens was built by being present. He isn't *any* Avan."

"Then, let's tell the queen. Maybe she can make a plan, too."

Placing her hand on the girl's shoulder, Sada smiled. "You know, it wouldn't hurt."

With Gabriel in tow, Edouard outstretched his wings and glided down a secluded pasture on Earth, near the remains of the Rosales farm. He set Gabriel on a fallen log with his bag.

The farm had been in ruins since the Garghons set fire to it and destroyed it years ago. Only the barn walls stood, the doors off their hinges, and the house crumpled into a heap of rubble indistinguishable from the debris littered across the lawn.

"I don't think it's a good idea," Edouard finally said.

Gabriel shook his head. "Sada wants some time to think."

Letting his wings disappear with the magic bestowed upon the Avans, Edouard sat on the log beside him. "So, the best thing is to leave Ava and come down to..." he said, examining the surrounding area again. A few flowers grew on the outskirts, where the road passed. The burned buildings to the Sevilla farm beyond stood where they should be. Mabon hadn't sold any of the land. They were ruins of a past never forgotten.

"You've come to find out if you can live without her?"

Pursing his lips, Gabriel scratched the surface of the log.

A splinter got lodged behind his nail, and he brought it to his lips. He shrugged his shoulders and watched the sunrise. The yellow hues painted lightly against a gray background, and slowly, the sky lit up in orange and blue. The moist grass under his feet smelled fresh and inviting. He used to run in the field as a boy. Tori bought him a kite once, too. It had two colored bows that he gave to his mother. He had never had one before. Yet, it was a past disappearing like the wind blowing his hair back.

"What do I tell Mabon?" Edouard stretched his arms. Toned and long muscles contracted.

A few birds flew past them, and their songs followed.

"*Por favor*, just tell him I'll be okay. The Rosales have been working for the Sevillas for a long time. All the secrets will always be kept in honor of that promise."

"And Tori? She won't like this."

"I know."

"I can't stop her from sending a party to find you."

"I don't think she would do that. Would she?" Gabriel turned to Edouard; his face skewed under the sun's rays.

"You two have been through a lot. Getting captured by the Garghons and being pecked at, then having your—"

Lifting his palm to stop the Avan, Gabriel said, "*Ya sé*. Just tell her she can always look through the water."

Feigning a smile, Edouard stood and stretched out his white-brown wings. His silhouette against the sunrise was a masterpiece like the ones Gabriel had seen on a field trip to the museum. Statues of nude Greeks in their prime.

"I must get back before my classes start, Gabriel, but know that if you ever need me, just say my name and I shall come for you. This is the gift I leave you."

Nodding, Gabriel extended his hand, and they shook. It was only for a second that the electricity from Edouard's grasp circulated to his arm. "Thanks, *amigo*."

With a last goodbye, Edouard took flight and glanced back only once before disappearing into the clouds. And all hope of Gabriel returning to Ava went with him.

CHAPTER
5

On his way to meet with his mother, Mabon caught sight of his sons exiting her study. Their faces were as forlorn as the day the rescued bird they tended died after days of caring for it. Mabon rushed toward them and kneeled in front of them.

"What is it?" He took each of their trembling hands.

"Queen Kalani asked us to come, and then she felt tired," Xander replied.

Xio added, "She doesn't want company right now."

Mabon lowered his eyes and wondered whether the side effects of the poison Ibis gave her were part of a bigger curse. It's been years since they drained the poison, but the queen continued to weaken—even aging differently than the rest of the Avans. He'd have to counsel Oda. Though, Oda had been avoiding him lately. Removing his hands, Mabon rose and looked at the closed doors to the study, where the two guards stood still, their armor gleaming, accentuating their broad shoulders. Surely, his mother had time to speak with him about her condition or about Tori's request to let the twins spend more time on Earth, but he didn't want to press it, especially since he knew she would rather have them prepare for their coming wings.

Turning back to his sons, he asked, "What news did the queen bestow?"

"Not much." Xio shrugged his shoulders. "Save the world and stuff."

Mabon placed his arms akimbo. "And I suppose you accepted such a fate?"

"Well, she struck a hard bargain." Xio moved his arms opposite each other with a tilt of his head.

Xander burst out laughing. Xio joined him, and the two almost bumped heads.

Mabon could only smile.

"Prince Mabon!" a voice boomed down the hallway.

The Sevilla's turned and spotted Quoba's approach. His sword and shield clapped against each other as he ran, and his finely sculpted muscles rippled with each step, but the look on his face was one of dread.

"My lord." Quoba bowed and touched his forehead, then lowered it. "You must come to the courtyard."

Mabon's smile faded as he neared Galeno's second in command. "What is it, my friend?"

Taking a deep breath, Quoba's eyebrows knit together. "King Waqar has broken through our barriers. His spirit wants to address you."

"Protect the queen." Mabon sprouted his large white wings, almost knocking down his sons. He bowed to the boys and said, "Don't leave the study. I'll let your mother know."

"I already did, father," Xander said, his voice cracking. He took Xio's hand. "We'll stay with the queen."

Xio had closed his eyes for a second, and when he opened them, he stated, "I don't like him coming here."

"Neither do I, son, but I must depart."

"Fine." Xio added, "I called Romeo to our side."

Mabon nodded to them, and Quoba returned the gesture as he relayed the message to the guards, and he flew down the corridor. Turning a sharp left, he signaled for the doors to open to the courtyard. Troops lined up for battle, their swords drawn. Some with spears at their sides or shields in hand.

Their gold and silver helmets and armor plates beamed with the Avan symbol: wings with a sword in between.

Half of the army surrounded the image of King Waqar for the first defense. The rest settled behind Galeno. Mabon landed beside him.

The Garghon king's laughter thundered in the open space. Only his large head took up the center of the courtyard. His twisted horns and sharp teeth terrified the Avans looking in from the terraces or behind trees.

"So, the prodigal son remained under the queen's command."

The whispers were silenced, and his hot essence singed Mabon's skin.

"Speak." Mabon's fists tightened, and his knuckles turned white. "Why do you intrude on Ava without a cordial invitation?"

"I don't need an invitation."

The prince's eyebrows shot up.

"And I will never adhere to your peace talks unless you give me what is rightfully mine."

"What's he talking about?" Tori had made her way past the guards to Mabon's side.

"Woman, you must step back." Galeno pressed the shield in front of her.

Tori met the Avan leader's piercing green eyes and fine nose. At first, she wanted to push ahead, but then she noticed her husband's concerned stare and agitated jaw.

Mabon motioned for her to stay behind. Once she stepped back a little, Mabon continued to address the king. "By breaking the code to speak on neutral ground, you dance on waging war."

King Waqar bellowed. He narrowed his fuming eyes and said, "If within three hours I do not have what I want, the Earth will experience the wrath it so much deserves."

As the image faded, Mabon reached for the creature's horns but only caught the mist.

Some Avans burst into unison in their displeasure, and some cried for peace. Others held their children in a tight embrace.

"This is absurd." Galeno sent two sets of guards to recheck the perimeter and another set to scout above for any other foul play from the Garghons. Then he addressed the prince, holding the pommel of his sword. "Queen Kalani would have to meet this challenge."

"Galeno, please..."

"Are you going to allow this violation to play out?" He closed the distance between them, head high.

"We have to look into what King Waqar means by dooming the world."

"So, while we research our prey, they proceed to prepare for their plans."

"He means to take my babies, Galeno," Tori intervened. "Your acting king only wishes to be informed before making hasty decisions."

"You dare?" Galeno raised an eyebrow. He had flawless skin and raven hair, which moved freely and securely, but his eyes alone could intimidate.

"This is just the beginning. Don't you see?" Tori approached the Avan leader. "They must have something to risk coming here."

"She is right."

Those gathered stopped and turned toward the collective, direct voice. The Avans hidden behind trees stepped out of their shadow. Oda hovered above them, alighting on the mound. His cloak waved like a flag, and the beard he had grown longer joined it.

"The Garghons hold in their possession an ancient text full of dark magic. The same one Ibis used to conjure up the spells that kept her alive."

"And the same book keeps the queen in her stupor." Camille appeared above the crowd in her dark green dress with waving sleeves and flew down after Oda. Her long black hair bounced off her shoulders. She was beautiful and determined. "We must get it back before the Garghons unleash havoc on Earth."

"We might be too late for that, dear," Galeno said. He approached his mate and kissed her hand. "They mean to slay us while we protect the world from whatever they unleash."

"This talk is getting us nowhere," Tori said in frustration. "What are we going to do to stop them?"

"If they have the book already, we may not have a choice in what we do." Galeno clutched his sword.

"Protecting the earth is our priority," Mabon said.

"Mabon?" Tori took a breath, and with her mouth agape, she covered it.

"The twins will get all the protection they need here," he reassured his wife, though he wasn't sure himself what the Garghons intended for Earth, and he wasn't going to hand over his sons to let Ava rot. The unfair gamble only provided three hours until the Garghons' next move, leaving little room to prepare for the onslaught.

CHAPTER

6

Staring at the large hotel sign where his brother rented, Gabriel dropped his bag and sighed. Maybe the idea was to avoid having his girlfriend's emotions jumble him on Ava, but really? *What was he doing here?*

Someone honked, and Gabriel moved out of the road toward the lobby entrance, inquiring about his older brother at the desk. The hotel staff didn't confirm or deny his staying there, so Gabriel walked up the stairs to the third floor. He wiped his sweaty palm on his jeans and knocked on the door.

Each second scraped against his skin as if a scorpion crawled on it. All the while, he rubbed his sweaty palm over and over again.

The footsteps were light and slow in the room. The latch for the lock was coming undone when, midway, it stopped.

"What do you want?" came the brusque voice behind the door.

Which meant Jaime must have seen him through the peephole.

"We need to talk."

"There's nothing to say."

Silence.

Jaime had been staying in the city for two weeks. Gabriel

knew this because Sada had looked into the water and pro-fessed it long before he arrived.

Gabriel stared at the door hinges, hoping his brother would open and at least speak to his face. They must have taught him that in the Air Force, right? Though it didn't make it better that neither of them had kept in touch after their parents' deaths.

After two minutes passed, Gabriel said, "I can camp out here."

Luckily, the door opened, and Gabriel met his brother's scowl and dark brown eyes. The same ones their father had, along with the large ears. He couldn't help but smile.

"What is it, Gabe?" He leaned his forearm against the doorframe, his lips sealing tight together.

"See if you're okay," Gabriel said softly.

Jaime looked at the bag his brother carried and asked, "What's that for?"

"Can you at least let me in so we could talk?"

"There's nothing to say."

"I tried calling..."

"¿Cuándo? Last year, when I was halfway around the globe on a mission?"

"Yeah. You could have returned my emails." He watched Jaime's eyes narrow. "You're the only family I've got."

Jaime sighed and motioned for Gabriel to enter, then slammed the door shut and crossed his arms. His hair was cropped short but not buzzcut, just enough to pass by.

"Look, you got to know Mom and Dad better than me, and now you want to come back after a long absence? *Mierda.*"

"I tried to see you, but you were never around." Gabriel lowered his eyes. "Or you had something going with the Air Force."

"Right. And I suppose disappearing from the face of the Earth helps in the matter?" He dropped his arms and stomped to the small kitchen counter. He placed his palms against the counter and pressed them against the edge. Turning, he said with irritation, "You've got some nerve showing up here."

"*No peleemos.*" Gabriel set his bag on the floor.

"Who's fighting?" Jaime shrugged his shoulders. "Me and you got nothing to say."

"Please, Jaime. I'm sorry..."

"Sorry doesn't cut it. Look at you!" He pointed to his brother, looking him up and down. "You look like you've trained for a triathlon."

Gabriel pulled his shirt down.

"Still can't tell me where you ran off to?" Jaime slammed his fist on the kitchen counter. "Get out!"

Stepping closer to Jaime, Gabriel said, "It's not like that, *muchacho.*"

"Just grab your stuff and go."

"You know I'm the gatekeeper."

"Yeah, yeah. You're so full of hot air like dad was about this secret keeping crap, you drown everybody out."

"I know you wanted to be—"

"Stop it!" He pushed his brother.

Gabriel fell back on his bag, then hit the floor with his elbow. A sharp pain traveled to his funny bone.

"Stop drowning me, Gabe."

Gabriel lifted himself up, but before he could explain what had happened to him these past years, an orange-purple form appeared against the wall. Gabriel covered his face as his brother turned to view the image of a large creature with charred wings. It had them spread wide open, encompassing the living room and filling it with a moldy scent.

"What the hell is that?" Jaime asked, keeping his mouth open.

The creature sent black rays from her hands toward Gabriel, knocking him further down on the floor. The dark rays sent electric shocks through his body until he grew still.

"Shit!" Jaime gulped and froze in place. "Magic."

This thing couldn't be real. Nothing his father spoke of

could be. They were just silly stories he used to tell them on the rooftop of the barn, pointing to stars and clouds in the sky, except now the stories were alive in his living room.

"What'd you do to my brother?" He massaged his aching throat.

The creature spread its wings further. They looked like the feathers were burned off. The odor penetrated Jaime's nose to the point where he had to cover it with his hand. He turned to his brother, who lay on the ground clutching his chest from the burn going through his body, like the worry at what the creature was doing etched through Jaime. By keeping his eyes fixed on the dark rays that burst on all sides from Gabriel's chest, he didn't notice the creature do the same to him, knocking him down onto his back. The jolt sent a spasm of pain to his thighs.

"Get away, Jaime," Gabriel said with clenched teeth.

"Where am I going to? If that thing could find you—" Jaime managed to prop himself up against the wall.

But neither of the Rosales brothers had a chance to exchange any more words. The creature raised its arms and sucked some of the air in the room to form a spiral on the ceiling that turned into a small whirlwind.

"What are you?" Jaime covered half his face. Dust particles hit his forehead.

The creature laughed and kept the whirlwind in place before letting it fall on the two brothers in sweeping scoops.

A heavy pounding hit their bodies, keeping them flat on the floor. Their arms lay flat open. Shackles appeared around their ankles, formed from the same air it used.

"What's that thing doing?" Jaime tugged on his shackle, but Gabriel lay motionless.

"This isn't the world I want to live in, Gabe."

Once the wind died down, the creature's face crinkled, and a slight smile formed on its almost non-existent lips. It was then that Jaime got a good look at the thing whose face resembled a gargoyle and a bat-like alien entity. Its horns stuck out from the top of its head like two crooked branches, and its body was dark like the texture of a bog person. It had talons for nails and the body of a woman wearing a full-body leather outfit.

Repulsed and mystified at the creature's magic, Jaime got himself up by pulling the long shackles with him and said, "Get out of my apartment."

The thing laughed.

It could have been the stupidest thing to say, but Jaime had never backed down from a fight.

"Your lack of knowledge is pathetic, mortal, but I will tell you who I am. I am Tamesis, the Garghon witch, and you are now my slave."

"No!" Jaime lifted his fists and saw them shackled together, too. Cross-eyed, he let out a grunt. "What do you want?"

"I've told you. You will do my bidding by starting to get your brother up."

Jaime looked down at Gabriel. His face smashed against the ground. Licking his dry lips and tasting the dirt that fell on them. Jaime grabbed Gabriel's arm and struggled to lift him since the iron was tight around his wrists.

"You know what this thing is, don't you?" he whispered in Gabriel's ear. "It followed you here."

Gabriel could only shake his head as he leaned his weight on his brother. The rays still sizzled on his chest. When he opened his eyes, he noticed the Garghon and stepped back. "What do you *really* want?"

"You know, that question keeps popping up." She curled her lips. "But the two of you are morsels." She walked toward them, knocking objects on the floor with her wings, her eyes never leaving them. Jaime watched as the model airplanes collapsed to the floor, his bottom lip quivering as each step pounded in their heads. But Gabriel knew the magic kept everything hidden from the outside walls, and help would not arrive.

Tamesis stopped in front of the tall window and drew the blinds closed. "Your brother will be my emissary, Gabriel."

"For what?" He met his brother's wrinkled forehead and glossy eyes.

"Ah. Only he would be conscious to know." She knocked Gabriel back down with the dark rays. They left her talons like rope and attached themselves to him, shattering the shackles.

Gabriel fell to his knees again and screamed from the agonizing energy.

"Hey!" Jaime got hold of the Garghon's arm but released his hold when he felt the snake-like texture of it.

"Call them," Tamesis said. "Call whoever brought you here."

Gabriel squished his eyes shut. The pain constricted his chest, scorching his body. Hyperventilating, he grabbed hold of his shirt and tugged, suffocating from the energy the Garghon fixated on him.

"What are you doing to him?" Jaime knelt next to his brother.

"Call them," she repeated.

"Call who?" Jaime's face creased in bafflement.

Gabriel pried open his eyes, his hand still on his chest. He looked at his brother's confused, angry, and scared face. The Garghons were up to something, and his brother was part of it, whether he liked it or not. Losing his brother to the Garghons was not an option, but he could never betray the Avans. He squeezed his fist over his chest and answered, "No."

The Garghon witch picked Jaime up by the scruff of his shirt and tossed him against the wall.

Jaime let out a grumble as the wind was taken out of his lungs.

She put her palms together. A sizzling sound emanated, and an orange mist filtered through her skin, coming together between her fingers. She used it to morph a sword with various spikes on its handle when she separated her hands.

"Then, we must do away with the trash." She raised the

sword and lunged toward Jaime, whose eyes widened, mouth agape, while trying to crawl away.

Gabriel reached for his brother and whispered Edouard's name.

CHAPTER
7

Quoba stood guard inside the queen's study in front of the main entrance, while Romeo stood vigilant by the revolving door. He wasn't sure where it led, but the queen insisted on its protection. The twins and the queen occupied themselves with a board game, though deep down they each harbored strong feelings about the Garghon king's visit. Xio, especially, had a hard time concentrating, his elbow propped up so his hand could hold his head. The boy kept pressing his palm to his temple as if scratching away a bad dream. Opposite him, Xander twirled the same game piece on the table, never using it. His eyes, strikingly similar to both Sada and the prince, made Quoba uneasy. No one else on Ava had bicolor eyes. He often speculated whether the queen's choice of mate had the trait.

Meanwhile, Queen Kalani had pulled her large chair between the twins. He could tell she listened intently to the conversation in the courtyard. Her head tilted slightly in that direction. The light of the above glass fixture coated her skin.

No word had yet come of Prince Mabon's meeting with King Waqar. His muscles tensed at the Garghon's name, and he held the shield tightly within his grasp. Scanning the floor and windows, he stopped and regarded the ceiling to admire the plexiglass tiles.

"Would you like some?"

Quoba lowered his gaze and set his sight on the tall glasses lined on the silver tray before smelling the rose petal perfume from Willa, the queen's personal attendant.

"There's no need to be with thirst." She presented the tray to him, her fingernails perfectly shaped in ovals and painted with a pink sheen.

He nodded and drank from one of the glasses, letting the water sashay down his throat like the image of Willa in the garden when he first caught sight of her. A rare vision during his patrol of the grounds. "Thank you."

She took the glass from his heavy hand and smiled.

As she walked past him, he closed his eyes and savored the way her hair brushed against his chest like a weeping birch tree.

"Some thoughts are best kept private, Quoba, or have you forgotten whose presence you are in?" Queen Kalani looked at him with a serious expression, followed by a playful smirk.

"Forgive me, my lady," Quoba said with a start, and he straightened his stance.

"No need. For one as valiant as you should have reprieve of your duties every so often."

Quoba gulped. No words escaped him. He had lost a wing from their battle with the Garghons and had been given another of a darker hue.

"Is it weird to have a new wing?" Xander asked.

"No," Quoba said, wondering if the boy could read his thoughts, too. "No, my lord."

"Do not pry, son of Mabon." Queen Kalani adjusted her jeweled necklace. "Quoba may have lost that which he was born with, but he will never be anything less."

"Thank you, my queen." Quoba bowed.

Willa watched as the Avan returned to pacing the room. His body was larger than most Avans, with biceps the size of melons and auburn eyes that burned with passion. Being within a short distance of him made her blush and grow hot under the ears. She loved the way his soft, tender lips moved when he spoke. Would his kisses feel the same? She almost knocked over the tray she carried as her thoughts were interrupted by Xio's anguished cry.

The boy fell off his chair and cradled his head. He kicked for a few seconds from the pressure before curling into a fetal position to control the spasms.

Without hesitation, the queen got on her knees and picked Xio up gently by the head. As she held him in her arms, she sensed a great energy vibrate from her grandson's body like a wave brought down on her shoulders. His dark eyes changed to a yellow-mustard color for a second. She turned to Xander and asked, "What is this? I sense a mixed bloodline."

"Oh, oh." Xander dropped the board game piece and knelt beside her. He took her hand, and she squeezed it.

Willa appeared behind the boy. "May I be of assistance, my queen?"

"Make a place for him over there," the queen said, pointing to the farthest side of the room. "Quickly."

Quoba had now stopped pacing and taken out his sword in preparation for any attack, while Willa arranged the spot for Xio. The kingdom hasn't been the same since Mabon returned to stop Princess Ibis from destroying Ava.

Romeo left his post, went to the boy, and licked his scrunched-up face.

Xio recognized the dog's hot tongue and opened his eyes. "He's here," Xio repeated. He balled his fists.

"What does he want?" Romeo asked through their mental link.

"He means he's in his head," Xander projected.

Shaking his head, Xio couldn't reply. He made fists, and

tears dripped from his eyes.

"Look!" Xander pointed. Something was moving on his brother's back.

Willa gasped out loud.

"Xander, stop it now." The dog pushed Xio until he could rotate him.

That was when Queen Kalani spotted stubs forming on the boy's back. "It cannot be." She rolled her sleeves up and pressed her palms on the bumps, feeling the vibrating sensation. "There is a need for explanation. Avans do not sprout wings this way; only Garghons do, but for now, we must stop it from happening."

Xander nodded. Closing his eyes, he took three breaths. When he exhaled, a halo-like mist formed above his head. It glowed white, then an arctic blue, followed by a cold that filled the room. He raised his arm and spread his fingers wide. He called for the locket's energy from the vault with his telepathy. A strange indigo-like hue made its way under the door and onto the boy's hand. Frost covered his fingernails, but Xander sensed a warmth loaded onto his body. He closed his palm and slammed it on his brother's back between the bumps. The frost residue covered the stubs, and within a few seconds, they shrank.

Xander fell back and breathed hard. His chest seemed to be confined in a small box, wanting to break open to get a lungful of air. Sweat covered his body, and his joints ached.

Romeo went to comfort him. He nuzzled his snout against his arm. *"Thank you, young prince. Rest while I tend to your brother."*

Still catching his breath, Xander nodded.

"All is well, my lady?" Willa covered her mouth, unsure of what had happened, except that Xander was able to quench Xio's strange collapse.

Quoba, still at the ready, went over and assisted the queen up onto her chair.

"Thank you, Quoba." She paused and watched Xio turn over from his ordeal. He used his elbows to keep himself up, and he bent one knee.

"Your headaches have become too pronounced, son of Mabon." The queen looked at her hands. "I apologize for being unable to thwart the malice, but it seems the two of you are harboring much more than we expected."

Xio's lips turned down.

"It isn't time for the half-moon for you to get your wings." The queen softened her eyes.

Xio finally sat up and looked toward his brother for assistance, only to find Xander tired from saving him.

"Do you wish to make a statement about this new phenomenon?"

Xio gulped.

"Go on, Xio. There's no need for secrets," Romeo said.

Xio shrugged his shoulders, and a sharp pain struck his spine. He let out a short cry, then stood. He kept his eyes lowered, and said, "I think I'm connected to the Garghons... ever since that day Princess Ibis took me."

The queen leaned forward and met the boy's eyes. "You are no different, Xio. This curse that travels with you will come to pass on your tenth birthday."

"How?"

Before she could answer, the doors burst open, and Mabon entered, followed by Galeno and Oda. The wise one could barely stay on his feet.

CHAPTER

8

Edouard appeared inside Jaime's apartment, surrounded by a bright white light. The light stung the Garghon's eyes, and she backed away, covering her face with the sword. Edouard stepped in and took in the room, the turned-over furniture, the two windows, and front door for exits, the brothers in need of attention from their injuries. The further Edouard went inside, the more he realized the Garghon was a female he had not met in battle before. Her outfit fit snugly around her charred body like dry mud fused to the skin.

Tamesis lowered her sword as the brightness waned. "Good," she said, "I like what I see." She used her weapon to trace an outline of the Avan's body.

The brown spots on Edouard's white wings were visible now. He faced the Garghon, his toned arms at his side, his wings pulled taut.

"Leave," he said.

She admired his strong hands gripping the bronzed staff, making his muscles flex. She only attacked head-on or from a distance. Now she wanted to check the Avan's stamina.

Edouard curved his wings back and materialized a longer staff with a spiked ball at its center. "You must be hard of hearing." He lunged forward and hit the Garghon on its shoulder.

Tamesis let out a wail and plunged her sword into him,

but Edouard was swift and moved away from the edge. She collided with a bookcase lined with plants. She licked her lips at his green-gray eyes under the light. Never had she seen an Avan with such weightless movement. Turning, she struck her sword on the Avan's staff.

Edouard smelled her hot, acidic breath and locked eyes with her. "Need a breath mint?" Then he pushed her back, striking her knee and forearm.

Jaime watched in shock as the two creatures struck blows. The room lit up in orange, white, purple, and lime. Smoke lifted from the floor as the creatures moved.

"Bet the S.W.A.T. team's on the way," Jaime remarked.

"Never mind that. The magic keeps the neighbors from hearing." Gabriel lifted himself up with the aid of the sofa's arm. "We've got to step outside where it's safe."

Jaime acknowledged and grabbed Gabriel's arm the best he could with the heavy shackles on their ankles and wrists. They chafed their skin as they moved. Stumbling after a few steps, Jaime stepped on Gabriel's foot and hit his head on the table's edge. Once up, they hopped and limped toward the door. When they reached it, they found the doorknob missing.

"She's keeping us here," Gabriel said. Sweat fell on his eyelashes, and he wiped it away.

"Great." Jaime looked back at the two magical beings hurling metal against metal. "I should have listened to *Papá's* stories. Maybe I'd be able to do something."

"There's not much we can do." Gabriel raised his shackled wrists as a reminder. Though he trained to protect himself with the Avans, it didn't help that the witch wasn't playing fair. Would this have happened if he remained on Ava? Where would his brother be without Edouard's aid?

Noticing his brother's deep-set eyes and frown, Jaime said, "Let's bust the door down."

Hearing her prisoners, Tamesis jumped over Edouard, landed behind him, and used the flat part of the blade to strike his back, briefly stunning him. She quickly turned to the brothers and said, "Not so fast." She waved her arm in a circle, manifesting a cloud, blasting them with a tornado-like wind.

The two brothers ascended to the ceiling. Their backs crashed against the bedroom wall before plummeting to the floor with such force that they were left winded and in pain.

Regaining his balance, Edouard raced to protect them, but the witch summoned another whirlwind, raising the Avan off the ground and plunging him across the room and out the door.

Edouard's back smacked into the hallway's wall, leaving an indentation. He slid to the ground and shook his head from the impact before standing. Ready to battle again, he collected his staff, but the Garghon had Jaime by her talons. She whispered in his ear and orange dust blew in them. Whatever it was, it could not be any good.

Edouard ran through the now open doorway and raised his staff to strike.

By then, Tamesis had let the brother fall unconscious to the ground.

"No!" Gabriel grabbed the creature's ankle, pulling her down as much as he could.

Growling, Tamesis looked down at the human and struck Gabriel with the pommel of her sword, knocking him out.

Leaping forward, Edouard struck the Garghon's thighs with the staff until she blocked the Avan's attack.

Their weapons tangled like snakes while a purple cloud formed around the Garghon. Tamesis smiled at his ability, and her sharp tooth stuck out. Hauling the Avan close to her, she said, "You're good, but not that good." She passed her cheek on his, savoring the smooth skin Garghons lacked. "Not yet, Tasty." She pushed away with her foot.

Edouard wiped his cheek. It felt like sandpaper had scraped against him. "You're not taking anyone."

She stood tall and spread her dark wings, wiped her

bloodied mouth, and addressed Edouard, "Next time, you won't be so lucky. I'm going to enjoy making you suffer for this delay, but right now, you have better things to tend to." She motioned her sword to the brothers before disappearing in a cloud of smoke.

CHAPTER
9

Mabon, Galeno, and Oda had entered Queen Kalani's study after King Waqar proclaimed his demand for Xio. Mabon took one look at his children next to Romeo, and he knew they were still not free of the Garghon's hold. His heart burned in his chest for not being there for them.

He needed to stop the Garghons before they could get too powerful and destroy his family, *and* before the twins underwent any more unexpected changes.

Scanning the room, Galeno noticed the twins on the floor with tired faces and the queen staggering next to his second in command.

"What has happened here?" Galeno addressed Quoba.

"Do not fret, Galeno." Queen Kalani waved. "Quoba has protected us with his gallantry. It is the children we must worry about." She called for her chair with a whiff of magic, and the large object made its way to her. She sat and turned to Mabon. "What is it you're not telling us?"

Mabon got on one knee and placed his forearm on the bent knee. "Your highness, King Waqar wants my son, or hence the earth shall perish."

"That is not what I asked, Prince."

Sighing, Mabon locked eyes with his mother. He was familiar with her tone. She wanted to see the children grow into full Avans. "The princes' magic has been summoned early, your majesty."

The queen held her breath for a few seconds before she veered toward Oda. "Is this sudden appearance by King Waqar connected to Xio's sickness?"

Oda bowed, almost stumbling forward. "Camille and I have gone over as many spells as possible that could have been used on the young prince. The only conclusion is that dark magic is at work." He materialized a staff made of dark wood and used it to balance himself. His face was as pale as someone who had never seen the sun. "The spells come from a book missing from the library."

"Dark magic has been banned from Ava, Oda."

"Yes, my queen," he said, bowing his head, "but Ibis had stolen the book and used it against us once before."

The queen gestured for another chair for the wizard. Watching her long-time friend was excruciating, but she had to contain her composure. These were trying times again, and the sudden strength Xander executed to stop the darkness must have an origin. "And this book will explain the princes' enhanced abilities?"

"That is the wish, dear Queen."

"Will it free Earth?"

Oda nodded. His eyes were puffy, and his lips were dry. He maintained a shallow breath as he sat. His glasses fell to the tip of his nose, and he removed them.

Rising, Mabon said, "This book... could it have a way to stop my son from transforming?"

The old wizard nodded again.

"Whatever this book is, we can't go off hunting for it while we leave Earth undefended, not to mention Ava without an elite guard," Galeno said in a rushed tone. He paced the room, passing his long fingers through his hair, letting strands fall on his forehead, and repeating the movement. He stopped in front of the queen and knelt. "My lady, King Waqar has breached

Ava." He raised his piercing green eyes, and the light above hit them, making them shine like a quartz crystal. "Though, he didn't say the words, he has asked for war."

"What you speak of is true, Galeno," Queen Kalani replied. She turned to her son. "What would your liege do at this dire moment?"

Mabon's jaw clenched, and his thumb rubbed his fingers. The duties he has been dealt have left a gaping hole in his side, as it was both an honor and a curse to have been born prince of Ava without the time to balance his life. He wanted to protect his family. Be the hero to both Avans and humans. *At what cost?*

"I have no choice but to meet the Garghons on Earth and protect it."

The door burst open, and both Camille and his daughter, Sada, entered in a flurry.

Sada rushed to the queen and kneeled in front of her, taking her hand and kissing it. "I'm so glad my lady is well."

Queen Kalani gestured and turned to greet Camille, whose face was white and whose eyes were wide with despair. "What news do you bring?"

Camille bowed and approached the queen. "Our news is most severe, my queen. Earth is undergoing violent weather-related and natural disasters as we speak."

Galeno rose suddenly, his fist wrapped around the handle of his sword, and said, "They break their promise as well!" Then, facing the prince, he asked, "What say you, my lord?"

Bringing his fingers to his chin, Mabon viewed the faces of the Avans in the room. It gave him a bitter taste in his mouth. His mother's forlorn face waited for his decision. Each day, she relinquished more responsibility to him. He could never return to being what his father was— tending the land and raising animals. Then Sada's saddened eyes met his. She understood what a burden he carried and would do anything to assist. She was of age, after all. Thus, her choice to follow in Oda's footsteps has made her stronger. Camille's unwavering hope would be a guiding light alongside his wife's. Galeno's determined fate and Quoba's patience would fight their opponents until Earth was safe again. Though the twins' disillusioned faces were eating Mabon and tearing at their desire to be free and choose their own destiny, they had come to Ava to learn and to live peacefully. If they're tied to the mystery behind King Waqar's request, then he has another battle to settle.

Mabon closed his eyes, and Romeo's short whine made him open them again. He caught sight of Willa's glum expression, holding the moist towel in her fist. The room seemed to spin. He stopped at Oda, who clutched his chest, coughing briefly, and shaking his hands.

"The book must be found." Oda lowered his hand. "Earth will need assistance. Ava will need defending."

"The Garghons must be held accountable." Mabon completed the thought.

Galeno punched the wall, denting the thick structure but feeling no pain since he was accustomed to the tough exterior of the Garghons during battle. "You can't possibly think the book holds enough to save us all."

"Restrain yourself, Galeno, or you will see the power of my words firsthand," Mabon declared in an authoritative tone he hardly used on his ex-mentor, but one he had to for the time nearing when he would be king, in spite of Galeno's aversion.

Galeno narrowed his eyes. Bowing, Galeno asked with gritted teeth, "And how do you propose to do this, your highness?"

"Camille will lead a small team to search for the book."

Camille lowered her eyes in acknowledgment.

"Quoba will lead an army to assist Earth."

Quoba removed his sword from its sheath, placed the central ridge on his forehead, and bowed.

Turning to Galeno, Mabon said, "You will defend Ava."

"Surely, your highness, you are not thinking of heading an

army to the Garghons front door?"

"Yes." Mabon turned to his mother for confirmation of his plans, but before he could, Oda collapsed on the ground.

CHAPTER
10

Baqir and Tamesis entered the bathing room located within one of the various volcano chambers. These were used for cleansing the body of particles that would stick to it, except today. They were empty save for the Garghon King. He was here, alone, and preparing his body for the final hour when the Avans would give up the prince. The king sat in a vat full of steaming water fueled by the lava flowing underneath.

This was the only place Garghons came to bathe, and both Garghon warriors had been summoned during a ritual not many have seen with their heads intact. Even the sentries flew around the outside of the volcano to not bother the King. Baqir and Tamesis waited for him to emerge from the water to relay the news of their exploits. Baqir, for one, kept tapping his foot on the rock floor, peering away from the king. The depths of the cavern were hot enough and the boiling water soothed their skin.

Though Baqir disliked the bath for being too far from their headquarters, it was built for safety. No one liked to be caught off guard without their weapons. Glittery walls and stalactites were the only things to see, and the ocean salt was better on the outside.

Baqir turned back to face the king, who finally surfaced from the vat to stand. His broad shoulders and thick deltoids were a constant reminder of why *he* was king, and Baqir knelt, awaiting his orders.

The water slid off Waqar's body like streaks of falling icicles, uncovering his dark skin. Stepping out of the vat, all the muscles of his gluteus and legs moved in sync.

Wiping the excess water from his face, King Waqar asked, "What news do you bring?"

Admiring the sight of the king, Tamesis knelt and replied, "Your most gracious sire, the human pest has been planted on Ava with the instructions as foretold."

She glanced again at the king's nakedness. As the huge Garghon turned, she couldn't help but lick her lips. Imagining his past appearance as a handsome muscle-rippled human or Avan. It only reminded her of the tasty white feathered Avan she recently battled. No one was sure of the king's true origin, only that he had fought two major wars with the Avans and lost a mate to the Avan queen's hand.

Garghons weren't allowed to have mates, which suited their war-like society. There wasn't a need for companionship when you were made of death and skipped childhood. If Prince Mabon never forced the king's hand to expose the Garghon origins, she wouldn't be considering having a mate, much less an Avan with skin so soft that if cut, it bleeds like juice from crushed berries.

The heat of the cave had dried the king's skin, and the last drops evaporated at the tip of his horns. "And you, Baqir?"

"Earth is already experiencing the worst."

"Good." King Waqar walked to the edge of the chamber, where the rays of the sun went through a slit opening above. He outstretched his arms and summoned his leather outfit. It appeared on the protruding rock beside the vat. "Queen Kalani cannot read your thoughts. No Avan can, as long as you maintain the spell." He materialized a long sword, lifted it up to the sun, and viewed the skewed writing on the pommel. "You know what to do?"

Baqir raised his head and answered, "Yes, your greatness. Prince Mabon will not be able to stop what's coming."

Oda's body fell to the floor like a feather floating in the wind. Mabon, being close, caught the wise one's shoulders, taking his weight with his upper body. Galeno took hold of his feet, and they placed him on the table.

Queen Kalani stood and wiped the tears from her eyes before they inched their way over her cheeks. She approached her friend's body and placed her hands above his chest, leaving an inch of space between them. She was out of breath at the sight of his bluish lips.

"He is gone," she said softly. Her hand remained in place, clutching his amulet.

"Impossible!" Galeno stated. "Send in one of the healers! That Declan..."

"Wait. What happened?" Sada asked as she flew closer. "Why has he fallen?"

"Oda has left us." Camille placed her hand on Sada's shoulder. "It was his time."

Tears flowed from Sada, and she gripped the straps to her chest plate. "No!"

She went to Oda's body and hugged it. She felt the warmth escape him, leaving behind a coldness of tiny ice particles. Her shoulders moved up and down as she wept, and her tears rolled onto him. He had said she was a great apprentice, as great as Camille, and now all that remained were the memories of those nights in his cottage, manipulating spells and potions. A tightness pressed over Sada's heart, surrounding her shoulders, and she realized she couldn't make her wings disappear. The tension burned across her forehead, and she screamed. Her hands were coiled around Oda without a means to get loose.

"What is happening?" Mabon tried pulling Sada off, but the appearance of a green glow intervened, pushing him away. He turned with concern to Camille. "What is it? Another Garghon curse?"

Camille turned her head away and sighed.

Xander stood from where he sat with his brother and said, "It's Oda."

Stunned, Camille turned to the boy. Their power grew by the day. Oda had been close to discovering the reason, even without the book. She asked for all to be silent as she reached Oda's spirit.

Sitting cross-legged on the floor, her body levitated and glowed brightly until her own life force floated and reached out. "Is it you, my colleague?"

The lights flickered.

"It is I," a voice resonated in the confines of the room.

Closing her eyes, Camille continued, "Come back to us."

"I cannot," the voice boomed. The Avans in the room covered their ears from the resonance. *"My wish is for Sada to take my spirit. Guide her. She will die if she fights it."*

"Why?" Mabon asked in a whisper and cracked his voice. "Why will she die?"

"It is fate."

Camille turned to the prince and explained, "During a merging of souls, the other must give in and accept, or else the pull would be fatal."

Shaking his head, Mabon watched as a bright blue cloud hovered above his daughter. Sada struggled to let go of her teacher's body, each time crying from the agony.

"Do as Oda wishes, Camille." Queen Kalani took Mabon's hand. Lines formed on her forehead from concern. Oda's spirit was wise and powerful. Sada was still young and growing. Her armband tattoos had gone. Only the Avan symbol rests below her ear and on her neck.

Mabon turned toward his mother's grip. Her small hand

weighed as much as a handful of oats, but her touch gave him hope, and he nodded. Time wasn't stopping for Avans or Earth. The Garghons could be using Oda's death to their advantage.

Camille lowered her lifeforce back into her physical body. She took a deep breath and massaged her aching head. When she managed to open her eyes, she walked to where Oda and Sada were. She positioned her hand on Sada's shoulder, clasping it, and pronouncing enchantments no other Avan understood but the queen.

The process would keep Sada out for a day until her strength merged with Oda's. The time for his departure seemed premature, but she trusted Oda. His powers would double Sada's, and she would be powerful in battle, for battle was where they headed. The queen squeezed her son's hand, and letting go, she gestured for him to speak.

"Avans," Mabon said, raising his right arm, "pick up your heads. Today we honor our greatest wizard by saving Earth from its catastrophes and bringing peace back to Ava." He lowered his arm and faced the Avans in the room, his eyes stopping at the twins. "And may the might of the flock be enough to bring balance to the four winds."

CHAPTER

11

Jaime woke up in a spacious room with high ceilings, angular lights, and glass windows carved like crystals. They reminded him of glaciers and how there were many facets in a diamond. *Where was he?* He blinked repeatedly as he heard voices. Whispers filled the cool room like a distant radio. He turned in their direction, and two women stood next to each other holding a large basin. They wore white scrubs and were beautiful, with radiant skin and full lips. A whiff of their powdery perfume reached him. Relieved he was in a hospital, he sat up and spotted his brother on the adjacent bed without covers.

"Good," he said to himself, letting out a puff of air.

One of the women noticed him and approached. Her white blouse was different from what he'd seen nurses wear. It had a V-opening collar, but it ran to the middle, where its hem tied crisscrossed to the back, creating a Greek goddess costume. She touched his arm with warm hands and smiled. "How are you feeling?"

"Not bad." He looked at the vacancy in the room and asked, "Where am I?"

"You're on Ava. It is not Earth." She took his pulse as if there was nothing wrong with what she said.

He looked at her in confusion, his heart throbbing to

the point of expansion. The crystals above seemed to move. "What? Where's Ava?"

"Never mind him," Gabriel said as he writhed in pain and lifted himself up.

She removed her hand from Jaime's wrist and smiled again. "We're the Healers who tended your wounds."

Gabriel massaged his shoulder as the other woman neared him and added, "Please, explain it. There isn't much time."

Gabriel nodded.

When the two women left the room, Gabriel sat on the bed and brushed his hair away from his face.

"This is the world *Papá* talked about?" Jaime viewed the ceiling and skewed corners in awe.

"Sorry you had to find out this way." Gabriel turned to his brother. "Ava is a world in the sky."

Darting his eyes, Jaime asked, "How should I take this?"

"Let me finish." Gabriel stretched but winced from the purplish bruises on his shoulders. "Avans are its people. They have a queen, and her son is Mabon Sevilla."

"So, this is where he went off to after that big fire?" Jaime pointed to the bare walls, which were a contrast to a barn's walls. "It's a long way from home."

"Yeah, the Garghons, that's the creature you saw earlier, destroyed it. The whole family's here. And from what I hear, the Garghons have made a move toward war."

"Great. Just great little brother, but I don't want to be part of any war." Jaime jumped off the bed but stumbled back from a short dizzy spell. His legs ached around his thighs, and he put pressure on them. "I'm not that kind of warrior."

"They're not asking for you to fight. They fight to protect Earth and their home." Gabriel pulled off his shirt and set it on the table next to the bed.

"Whoa." Jaime saw all of the bruises on Gabriel's torso. His chest was scarred with claw marks, as if he were in a boxing match. *"¿Qué diablos te pasó?"*

Sensing Jaime's shock, Gabriel disclosed, "I was almost killed five years ago." He traced the scar over his heart and closed his eyes at the memory of what Nafuna did to him when they captured Tori, the twins, and his own family. It was an injury the Avans were unable to remove and one that reminded him of his lack of Avan magic. Gabriel opened his eyes and met his brother's intense stare. "Garghons don't really care who they hurt as long as they win."

"So, why are you here?" Jaime raised his hands and let them down fast on his lap again, making the jeans sound like clapping at contact.

Gabriel lowered his eyes.

"Fine, little brother, but if you want to know what that thing told me before I rolled over, I can't. I don't remember anything."

"*Ya lo saben.*" Gabriel took the shirt and semi-folded it on the bed. "Edouard said you might not remember. Either way, they want you to be their guest."

"I'm not staying here," he scoffed.

"I know you don't understand what's going on, but you have to stay safe."

"Why? Can't bear to lose another family member?" Jaime stepped away from the bed, intently glaring at his brother.

Gabriel turned away, closed his eyes, and recalled his mother's face when the Garghon slashed at her and the way his father's twisted body hit the ground. He gulped and walked toward the glass window, hardly lifting his feet. He stood there, pensive. If only Jaime knew what the Garghons really could do if they were allowed to get away. If only Jaime had listened to their father about the secrets passed down to him.

"There's no way off Ava without the help of an Avan." Gabriel turned. "With your military background, I'm sure you understand what that means."

"I'm grounded. I get it."

Gabriel picked up his shirt and made his way to the door.

"Now, where are you going?"

Gabriel stopped short of the door and clutched the shirt. "You might find it hard to believe, Jaime, but I'm going to help any way I can."

The doors opened, and Gabriel walked out, leaving Jaime alone in the room.

Jaime looked down at his hands and made fists. He closed his eyes, and a pulsing started on his left temple. He massaged it, and then he heard something, almost a whisper, faint. He raised his eyes, but no one was there. The only feeling he had was that he had no choice about what he needed to do. His heart sank at the empty feeling forming inside him. His brother was going to war with monsters and flying people. *Why? Did either of them have a choice?*

"Jaime?"

Jaime turned and spotted the man who had fought the creature in his apartment. With a sigh of relief, he limped back to the bed and leaned against it. The man's wings were gone, and under all the immensity of the room, the contours of the Avan's body complemented the subtle white and beige hues painted on the walls. That's when it dawned on Jaime that this race might be made up of beautiful people. The nurses, this Avan, Mr. Sevilla—they all belonged on the front cover of magazines. Not only were the Avan's cheeks flawless like Mabon Sevilla's, but he also had a dimple.

"Does anybody wear a shirt around here?"

The Avan laughed and approached Jaime. "Since I was the one responsible for bringing you here, I have the great pleasure of escorting you to—"

"You're here because my brother won't introduce me to his new home, right?" Jaime cut him off.

"If you want to make this unpleasant, I can arrange that, too." He crossed his arms.

Jaime stared at the man before him. He wore brown pants that showed off the muscles of his legs and no shirt. A tattoo painted on his pectoral had two wings and a sword. The same tattoo as on Mr. Sevilla.

"I'm not gonna fight with you. I know what you can do." Jaime waved his hand in dismissal.

"Then, you know, I can't stay and play nursemaid. I'm a teacher, but at the moment, Ava is under pressure to attack the Garghons, and we're already one down."

"So, who's looking after me?"

"Prince Mabon's wife will deal with the details. She waits for you in the secure room."

"Great," Jaime said in a sardonic tone.

"I'd love to give you the tour, but..."

"But you've got a war to fight."

He walked past Jaime and stopped by the doorway. "And if you want to know, my name is Edouard. I will make sure your brother returns to you alive, whether you want him to or not."

CHAPTER
12

Baqir watched from miles away as the Avans dispersed from their home under the enormous cloud, which moved opposite the others. They were followed by the half-prince Mabon and another large warrior. This left the queen inside with the twins. *Perfect.* He crawled on the rock from the highest mountain top and scraped along the surface like a cat in search of its prey. He bided his time until the last of the Avan group flew down to Earth. Blowing on a silent horn made out of the carcass of a bighorn sheep to summon his warriors, Baqir trotted down to meet them. They crept out of their hiding places and presented themselves before him.

"There are two rooms I want intact," Baqir said as he stood and paced in front of them.

Garghons had no need for armor like the Avans because their skin was thick and rough. They didn't hide their wings from others, such as humans, but they wore similar pants and carried weapons of all kinds. His personal favorite was a spiked, round ball and chain that cut through skin and crushed the bones of his opponents. It gave him the ability to wrap the six-foot chain around them when extracted from the ball's core to hang them from a high spot. He reached for the morning star strapped to his back and clapped it down on his palm without wincing. The spike inserted itself there, blood trickled out, and the Garghons exhaled in awe.

Baqir stopped pacing, pulled out the spiked ball, and pointed it at them. "The room where Queen Kalani is, and the one where the twins are, must be intact."

"How will we know?" one asked. His teeth were filled with grime.

"They would be the ones protected by Galeno and his elite team. They wear silver and golden helmets."

The Garghons used their clubs to make noise by hitting the ground at the mention of the Avan leader's name.

"We'll roast him for dinner!" one called out.

"He'll pay for killing our brothers and sisters!" said another.

"And the rest?" A younger Garghon stepped out of the line. His charred wings glistened.

Baqir licked one of his long canine teeth and narrowed his eyes. He turned to the Garghons, one by one, and paused a foot away from the last one who had spoken. "I don't care about the others." Baqir's nose twitched in repulsion, and his yellow eyes in slits moved left and right. "Do as you please with them." And he slapped the warrior across the face with the back of his fist.

When an Avan dies, their spirit leaves the body. Rarely does it enter another's body to live in, as Oda's did. Queen Kalani didn't have the chance to recite a death farewell when she witnessed his demise. Camille could have easily taken his spirit, but the queen had a feeling Oda wanted Sada to be knowledgeable of what was to come. Her youth made Sada strong enough to deal with it. Though she feared what would transpire with the Garghons. Her son led the Avans to their stronghold. A trap perhaps. Were Earth's natural catastrophes a way to lure them away from Ava? What was King Waqar really up to? Her son had battled with the king before, and he must again. Yet her strength continued to fail her after all these years.

She turned Oda's amulet over in her hand. She had forgotten she held it tight. Its impression pressed on her palm. The light from the skylight above made the stone in the center gleam as blue as his eyes. When Oda's spirit left him, his body turned to ashes immediately and blew away on its own to cover the four winds. She would cherish the memories of the wise wizard, for there was nothing to bury. Now, Sada slept here, his spirit coursing through her veins until she could handle the power bestowed upon her.

"Does my lady wish to rest?" Willa asked, her voice cracking on the last word.

"This is not the time to rest, Willa." She rose from her chair and spread her wings. They reached the castle walls on opposite ends, sparkling under the light. It felt good to release them after keeping them concealed. "Bring my bowl."

Willa viewed the feathers' splendor and bowed.

Queen Kalani lowered her wings, bending them at the crest. They were heavy on her back muscles as time went on. "I want to see what becomes of my Avans and give them a helping hand."

"But Sir Galeno said you must remain safe." She placed her fingers on her lips, worried that the queen would insert herself into the battle. The Garghon King entered the courtyard without much trouble to threaten the prince. What would stop other Garghons from reaching these castle walls?

"I know what you think, dear child, but the Garghons haven't perfected their magic to enter unannounced again, nor have they bested me yet." She reached for the servant's hand and grasped it.

Willa nodded but remained silent. She was her queen, and Willa could only obey. A task in which she took much pride. Removing the drapes around a small box, Willa separated the bowl, a simple wooden spiral made of red oak. The bottom had been sanded smooth. She set the bowl on the small table and stepped back.

"My queen," Galeno walked in with his two elite guards, "News has arrived that Earth is experiencing strange weather in remote locations not conditioned to their aftermath." He stopped when he looked at the bowl. "What is happening here?"

"This is a potential coffin," Queen Kalani said, pointing to the room. "I won't wait to die locked in a room, and neither will the others."

"But your highness, the Garghons are dividing the flock on Earth. We must remain united to fend off the coming enemy."

"Fend off is what we'll do, Galeno." The queen had Willa pour water into the bowl. "I want this wall knocked down so the children can be near me."

"Is it not best to keep you hidden?" Galeno neared the queen. His eyebrows knitted together, and his shoulders slumped. "What if something were to happen to Prince Mabon?"

"The Garghons will not take the future legacy of Ava." She took his strong hands in hers and cupped them together. "You are bound to protect them at all costs, Galeno."

He sought to find reasoning in her eyes but only found determination in her touch, so he nodded and bowed.

"No matter what the cost," she repeated.

He gulped, his eyes jittering, but he could not voice any more opinion over what she asked him to do.

Beyond the kingdom's clouded barrier, a strange sound traveled through the trees, whispering. Willa followed Galeno's and Queen Kalani's eyes and looked through the window, her eyes wide with horror and her cheeks flushed in red as the chorus of sound increased to raucous battle cries.

"They are here!" She pointed.

CHAPTER
13

Romeo sat next to Urmi while the twins walked back and forth in front of them in the confines of the safe room. The only exits were the double doors etched with vines. Urmi braided three pieces of cloth and measured them around Romeo's neck. Avans weren't accustomed to having pets, much less having a dog around. After a few weeks, Romeo came to symbolize the twins' guardian. She hugged the dog, and as she did, Prince Xio stepped on her toe.

"You're not helping by doing that, you know?" Urmi pulled her hair back with a clip and continued braiding the cloth. "My mother says we have to protect Ava, not make holes in the ground."

Xio stopped and met her eyes. "I thought your father was doing that?"

She narrowed her eyes, not understanding, and wrinkled her nose.

"You know?" he continued. "Protect Ava."

Xander raised his hand before Urmi could reply. "She's right."

"Of course!" Xio slapped his forehead. "You would side with her."

"It's not that." He shifted his gaze to the side, and the three children turned to Tori. She had been trying to explain things to Jaime Rosales, Gabriel's brother, about what happened to the farm. Jaime was different from his brother, though. Xander could tell by the way he moved, sulking and rounding his shoulders, as someone who had been in the Air Force should do, and the way he talked... There wasn't much accent or emotion like Gabriel's. He also sensed something eating at him from the inside, like cancer spreading over his veins. Xander wanted to browse his mind further, but Xio elbowed him.

"Don't you think what Edouard explained is strange?"

"Ooh, you mean about the Garghon witch attacking his apartment?" Urmi fiddled with her dress straps. "How did she know where to find him?"

"That crazy book, remember?" Xio leaned on the wall. He crossed his arms and sighed.

"But look at the way he keeps his eye on us?" Xander leaned on the wall, too.

Xio rolled his eyes. "What can *he* do?"

"'Underestimating your opponent would be foolish,'" Urmi relayed her father's words to them. She tied the braided cloth around her waist.

They looked at the young Avan. She was the daughter of a sorceress and a military leader. Her future was set, whereas theirs had begun, and Xander knew they were destined to remain on Ava and follow in their father's footsteps. They only had to sharpen the use of their powers so that one day they might rule with wisdom and not force.

"I don't trust him," Xio said.

"You don't trust anybody," Urmi added.

Xio curled his lip and shook his head, mimicking Urmi's comment. He didn't like being confined in the room without the liberty to step out, and the girl wasn't helping.

But Xander focused on Jaime's eyes. Something was there—something dark—and he needed to get his mother away from him before something happened.

Tori transferred her weight onto the chair. "That's as much

as I can tell you in such a short time, Jaime." She stood and stretched her arms. Every muscle ached from the tension of waiting for the inevitable attack by the Garghons. "I hope you don't think your brother abandoned you. He fights inner demons as well."

"You sound like them," Jaime said, looking up at her with a twinkle in his eye.

Tori shook her head. "No, it's common sense. The Garghons want my children to get rid of the Avans."

"Sounds too simple." Jaime rubbed the nape of his neck.

"It's not," she reassured him.

"But why?" His face was flushed. "Are they trying to prove something?"

"It's so they could take over the Earth, possibly the universe."

He sat up and looked around the room. The walls had beautiful drawings of various birds, especially peacocks with ornate feathers.

She sat back down, leaned forward on the table, and placed her hands under her chin. "But we don't know what they want the children for, and all we can do is sit around and wait."

"Mom!"

Tori shot up. A bugle or some type of horn sounded. "Romeo, by the door." She hurried to her sons' side. "It could be anything."

"The gentiles are seeking shelter while the warriors assemble." The whites of Xander's eyes showed as he spoke in a monotone voice.

"Sometimes your gift scares me," Tori told Xander while her heart raced inside. She wanted Mabon to be the one protecting them, but he had to be the one to go to the Garghon stronghold, and Galeno had stepped out to check on the queen. She had to keep it together for the sake of everyone.

"Yeah, 'gentiles'?" Xio scoffed.

"But it isn't just anything," Jaime said. His brown eyes

turned yellow like the Garghons. "Hand them over." His voice was deeper.

Tori shook her head repeatedly, as if what she saw was part of a dream. *What's happening to his face? His voice?* Her chest tightened. This was Gabriel's brother. She had seen him on the farm when he visited from the Air Force with a big smile, making jokes, and eating double what his mother made him.

Without hesitation, Romeo left the door and jumped on Jaime, knocking him down and keeping a tight grip on his shirt's collar.

"*Good boy, Romeo. Keep him there,*" Xio said to their dog telepathically.

Jaime wrestled to break free. He pulled on the dog's collar and pounded at his foot.

Romeo kept a tight grip on him, though.

"Let them come peacefully, please." He heard himself say it while his body tried to get the dog off him.

"He doesn't know what he's doing," Xander said.

"The Garghon witch must have placed a spell on him before she left," Urmi said.

"The question is whether we could stop him from following the orders or not?" Xander added.

Tori brought her hands to her head and flattened her hair to keep from screaming. *Not again.* All she wanted was for her children to be safe on Ava*, but they'll never be safe as long as the Garghons crave the boys.*

"Doesn't matter." Xio pulled out a small dagger from his pants leg.

"What's that for?" Tori asked, taking the dagger away. Her hand trembled. The last time she held one in battle was when King Waqar's warriors had them surrounded and she needed to protect her sons. She turned it over and noticed the blade engraved with feathers and the grip handle with the Avan symbol. "Where did you get this?"

"We're not kids anymore, Mom. Not on Ava."

"No. No." She threw the dagger aside; it slid under the chair.

"He's right, Princess Tori," Urmi said as she picked up the dagger and turned it over in her hand. The blade shone like a gemstone. "They have a duty to perform, just like Romeo is doing now."

Tori closed her eyes and massaged her throat, which tightened at the thought of her children battling these creatures again. They were four years old when their powers awakened. It's unusual for an Avan to build that much power so young. Mabon had tried repeatedly to explain, but it happened. Oda ventured on a possible note that the powder Nafuna spilled over them had enhanced their abilities, and once the book was found, the spell could be controlled. She feared for Xio's power most of all. She knew he held back because of what Mabon's ex-mate, Ibis, tried to transform him into. Was that why King Waqar wanted him so badly? To finish the transformation spell so Xio could become their weapon? Tori let go of her throat and turned to Jaime.

Jaime bit Romeo's leg and pushed him aside. His eyes were darker, and his cheeks sagged. "I don't want to hurt you." His arm hung down while the other twisted in front of him. His leg followed the same motion until his body corrected its posture.

Romeo growled and bared his teeth.

Xio stood next to him and petted his raised fur. "We're not supposed to go with strangers."

"I don't think this is the time for jokes," Xander said.

Jaime's body convulsed, his skin darkened, and two one-inch horns appeared where his hair met his forehead. "I feel strong." He turned to the boys and reached for them.

"He's possessed!" Urmi threw the dagger at Jaime, stabbing him on the bicep. He pulled the dagger out and weighed it on his palm before preparing to throw it back.

Tori pulled the girl aside as the dagger ran past her cheek.

"Xander! Can't you slow him down?"

"I'll try." The young prince extended his arm and gritted his teeth. A purple light covered his arm, pulsing like a beacon and changing to a brighter blue.

"Oh, no, you don't." Jaime lifted a table and tossed it at Romeo before he jumped on him, then grabbed the chair and slammed it over the boy.

"Stop!" Tori let go of Urmi and ran toward Jaime, knocking him down with her weight. She began punching him. Her knuckles felt the impact on his face, making each blow cause her fingers to go numb from the pain. "He's just a boy!"

Jaime laughed, and his eyes burned orange. He seized Tori's wrists and said, "Hand them over before you get hurt."

She saw his eyes return to brown, struggling against the spell, and Tori refused to believe Gabriel's brother would hurt her, but he squeezed her wrists tighter, and she couldn't move her hand.

"My son is bleeding!" Tori pushed her elbows closer and used her forehead to butt Jaime's forehead. Once he released his grip, she got free and shut her eyes from the pain. Then, she continued to slap him at various places.

The young Avan reached Xander to check on his bleeding head. Urmi tore off a piece of her fairy dress and pressed it on the injury.

Xio aided Romeo from under the table. *"What do we do?"*

"You have to help your mother," Romeo said, panting. *"Be careful."*

Standing, Xio walked toward Jaime and his mother, his dark eyes turning into an empty void, blacker than the blackest hole in space. "Leave my mother alone, creep." A breeze blew his hair out of place. It came out of nowhere and filled the room with cold air.

Jaime pushed Tori off him and placed his elbows behind him to keep from falling. He wiped his mouth and said, "Good." His smirk showed an elongated tooth.

As the wind blew stronger, objects around the room flew in different directions, almost hitting Jaime. It went in the direction of a circle around the room.

Tori covered her head as a picture frame flew past her. Then she realized what was happening: Xio could become that which she feared. Stumps pushed Xio's shirt off his back, and his eyes hadn't returned to their normal color.

Urmi found the dagger among the littered papers on the floor and gave it to Tori. "Here, you must use it."

"No." Tori looked at the bloodied dagger. Her hand trembled at the sight of Xander lying motionless by the broken chair.

Jaime laughed louder, and it echoed with the wind.

"You must, Princess Tori." Urmi placed her tiny hand over Tori's; her large green eyes grayed. "Xio can't stop it."

Tori gulped and took the dagger. She felt the weight of its body and let it drop in front of her. She ran toward Xio, wanting to hug him to stop him from destroying everything. Already, the windows had shattered, and the ceiling began to rip open.

Xio's magic pushed her back, letting Tori fall on top of Romeo's leg.

Romeo whelped and licked his paw.

Jaime picked up Xander from where he lay and turned to Xio. "Come on, boy. Open the door!"

Sparks shot from Xio's fingertips, and he formed red lightning with them. Raising his arms, he hurled them at the door, bursting it open. The wood splintered, and the Avan guards fell on their knees, covering their ears as the impact crushed their eardrums.

"Good." Jaime took hold of the dagger, but Urmi bit his hand.

He let Xander fall on top of her as he stepped back from the pain. He grabbed the broken table leg and spat. "Too late, girl."

Urmi covered her face, but Jaime laughed and turned to hit Xio over the head with the pommel of the dagger instead. All the objects fell to the ground along with the boy. Jaime picked both twins up and made his way down the hall.

"Romeo..." Tori managed to open her eyes. "Romeo, after them..."

Romeo limped forward and ran after the twins.

CHAPTER
14

Gabriel wanted to turn back and find out what really happened to Sada, but the Avan army was close to Earth. Quoba issued the order to fly down and land in a desolate section of Yosemite Park that wasn't experiencing weird weather due to the Garghon's spell. Strange, since Yosemite was an ecological landmine and he expected it to be a place of chaos. Edouard took it upon himself to escort Gabriel down to Yosemite since Gabriel didn't have wings or magic to get there. *What was he doing?* He was human. Some Avans reminded him of this fact during his stay on Ava. Their narrowed eyes watched him slip and disliked the wins he got in practice. Some turned up their noses for daring to sit next to the princess during a demonstration. The two Avans who spoke to him mentioned Sada had to stay behind at the castle to recuperate from Oda's death. Nothing about defending the castle.

Beyond the vastness of the land, Gabriel watched Quoba divulge further instructions to the team.

"Maintain the catastrophes wreaking havoc on Earth from killing humans and animals." Quoba paced further into the circle the team formed. "So far, the casualties are minor and the Garghons have not been seen, but it's important to contain the magic thrown at the inhabitants."

The Avans responded with their warrior chant, and Gabriel followed the wind's breeze to the tops of trees.

"Are you well, my friend?" Edouard set Gabriel down on a small mound.

The smell of grass filled Gabriel's lungs, welcoming him, and from the corner of his eye, a furry critter scurried past them. He couldn't make out the species. Though, in the far distance, gray clouds made their way toward them, and the wind kicked up, pushing his hair toward his face.

"I will be when my head is focused on the fight," Gabriel said, sighing.

"Prince Mabon didn't dispute your wanting to join us." Edouard glanced at the coming dark clouds with worry. "We appreciate the help, but do you think it wise?"

The wind ruffled Edouard's feathers like cornstalks under the rain.

Gabriel knelt and pulled some grass blades, rubbing them on his palm. The scent of fresh lawn reminded him of his home on the Rosales farm when the grass cutting tractor traveled across the yard—a symbol of a fresh new start. He rose and squinted at the sun on the horizon, half-covered with clouds that looked like gray paint smeared on an orange canvas.

"You mean because my brother is on Ava?" He let the wind carry the grass away.

Edouard tilted his head, raised his eyebrow, and noticed the Avan warriors forming a line below. "This isn't going to be any ordinary fight."

"I know, *pero*... I want to. The Sevillas have done much for me already."

"Sada loves you, Gabriel." Edouard placed his hand on the young man's shoulder. "Give her some time."

Shaking his head, Gabriel said, "I love her, *mucho*, but..."

"Those aren't clouds!" an Avan pronounced, waving a blue and white flag. "They come as last time!"

"Avans on the ready!" Quoba commanded. He turned to

Gabriel as he placed his helmet back on. "Are you prepared, my friend?"

Nodding, Gabriel adjusted his helmet, too. The clouds in the distance looked darker, and the scent of coal or burned timber neared them. They heard the Garghon's laughter at the front. The cloud had a dim glow surrounding it.

"It's her," Edouard said in an ominous tone as the chills tingled his spine and ran down his fingers.

"Remember, if the Garghon witch has a taste for vengeance, call on us. Don't tackle her alone." Quoba raised his sword as a signal and looked at the teacher. "That goes for you, too." He turned to Gabriel before he lowered the sword so the Avans could disperse.

"That's one tip I *will* remember." Gabriel pulled out his sword and tapped his helmet.

"Good, because those clouds are getting bigger," Edouard added. Materializing his club, his chest tightened like frost around a lake.

The sky darkened as night painted its way across the horizon in an ink wash. After a few minutes, a tornado-like cloud appeared some miles away. Then it dissipated, revealing the Garghon army and Tamesis in the lead.

Far away, an island stood alone and desolate, but inside its newly awakened volcano, King Waqar sat on his throne, the top of his wings curled forward to match his pensive mood.

"They approach, King Waqar," a Garghon assistant said and bowed.

The king flew through the crater, and the Garghon followed. He stood atop the volcano's vent, one foot on the rock and the other on the loose dirt. He looked on at the Avan flock splitting in two, and he grinned. Scratching his chin, he caught sight of Prince Mabon flying toward the island. His majestic armor and huge wingspan distinguished him from the rest.

Though he knew the prince came solely for the Dark Magic Book to prevent Earth's total devastation and to help his family, he looked forward to a rematch with the half-human. It amused him that the prince was unaware of the capture of his twin sons and that they were on their way. His grin widened, and a single tooth protruded from his lips.

"Get the Garghons ready."

"Yes, my king," said the servant.

"Prince Mabon will die this day," he said in a soft voice, and crossed his arms.

"Do you want us to lead him to you?" The Garghon hunched over and backed up.

King Waqar glanced at the servant; his yellow eyes brightened. "He won't come willingly, fool!"

The volcano shook, and smoke snaked its way past them while the sulfur buried their feet like dust clouds.

"Gag him. Tie him. Drag him to me." The Garghon king turned to the minion and grabbed its jaw. "Kill as many Avans as needed to get him to comply."

CHAPTER
15

A strong wind circled the Avan team Mabon led, concealing them five miles away from the Garghon Island stronghold. Salt and smoke packed Mabon's lungs as Camille conjured the proper spell. They drifted over the clear ocean; rocks, fish, and plants were a mirror to another world far different from that on land. Once he raised his eyes, Mabon noticed Camille hold her fingers on the sides of her head; her long, wavy hair flowed like tides on the ocean surface, and the red highlights sparkled along with the red cloud she stood on. After several minutes, she lowered her arms and turned to Mabon.

"The book is inside, my lord, but guarded by a large beast."

"A beast? Why would Garghons need a beast?"

"It is the book's guardian, named Aja," she said in a dire tone.

Mabon neared her, gliding past two sentinels. "How did the Garghons use the book and keep the beast at bay?"

"Dark magic doesn't work the way you think, your highness. Aja had to be summoned by crossing the west with the east wind, which isn't easy to do, especially when Aja is a—"

"What you're saying is that we were expected?"

She nodded and raised her arms. The cloud she stood on was elevated out of the wind surrounding the Avan sentinels. Their armor shone under the light of the moon and the sun's distant rays. Their myriad-colored wings flapped with the air blowing around them. She turned toward the island and allowed the wind to die.

"On your command, my lord," she said, forming a staff with the head made out of an emerald blade.

Mabon nodded and gestured for four female warriors to follow Camille, and the rest followed him. Fashioning his own sword, the prince heard the splash of a whale in the distance and the roar of the ocean calling his name, but he had no time to contemplate nature.

"Make sure the beast returns to the book, Camille." Mabon waved for the soldiers to prepare. "We'll hold off any interference."

"Yes," she replied. She flung the red cloud out of the way. "King Waqar most likely awaits your return, my prince."

"He waits for the heir to Ava and will regret his threats."

With that, the Avan soldiers behind him raised their weapons, wings fully open, and with determined faces saluted the prince and adjusted their helmets for battle, which soon was accompanied by the cries of Garghons carried by the wind.

The Garghons gathered above the volcano. Their cries continued to echo, and their dark wings flapped fiercely, causing them to sound like a swarm of giant bats.

Mabon spotted them and sent two more warriors to aid Camille. She had to enter their domain to collect the book. Its dark magic had to be sealed to prevent further damage. He turned back to the Avans behind him and gave them the signal to halt.

Soaring ahead, Mabon landed on the shoreline; his feet sinking into the wet sand reminded him of his ordeal years ago. He had fought the Garghon King and barely made it out alive. Oda came to his rescue and healed him. Oda wouldn't be there to heal him if things went this time. Mabon looked around for Garghons, but they all seemed to concentrate above. He sheathed his sword and moved up the shore to the drier part of the beach. Unlike most beaches, the scent of salt was covered by the stench of burned flesh and blood. It lingered in your nose and settled in your gut like a nauseous liquid.

The wind blew Mabon's hair back, and he called out, "Waqar!"

The breeze blew stronger, pushing him back to the wet sand. Slipping, Mabon stopped himself from falling back into the ocean with his knee and fingers. He raised his dual-colored eyes, and a figure stood ten feet away. It wasn't King Waqar's huge body and horns. A brown creature with small horns stood there with its wings fluttering. Mabon got up and drew out his sword, and as he did so, the Garghons above landed on the beach. Their yellow eyes narrowed, their weapons were held firmly, and their motives were written on their wrinkled faces. Without further delay, he gestured for the Avan warriors to come down.

One by one, the Avans plunged to the ground, ready for the inevitable. The Garghons didn't wait for any cry or order; they saw their adversaries and ran toward them. Mabon struck one on the forehead with the edge of his sword and watched the agony in its eyes with satisfaction as he removed the blade. War had a way of bringing out the worst in people, and he was no exception. Neither was the time to judge himself when he had to get Camille inside to retrieve the book and stop the catastrophes happening on Earth before more people and animals died. Maybe even put an end to his sons' torment.

Garghons and Avans broke their circle and lines and violently attacked each other from all sides. Swords, chains, clubs, and spears clattered and drowned out the waves surrounding them. Mabon struck down many creatures and made his way to Camille's team, who were fending off those who prevented their entry to the volcano.

"They appear from nowhere!" one warrior said.

Camille twirled her staff above her head; the emerald stone grew bright and formed a green circle. It spun higher without the aid of the staff and landed on top of the Garghons, knocking them off their feet and dispersing their formation. Their weapons fell from their grips, and the Avans picked them up to continue warding off the creatures away from the entrance Camille was to enter.

Severing a Garghon's horn, Mabon relinquished command to an elite warrior with hair as golden as the Autumn sun reflected on a clear lake's surface and pushed himself forward in the formation. Butting another Garghon, Mabon got behind the line of defense the women made.

Camille charged through an opening amidst the dispersed soldiers to the entrance and leaned against the rock before entering. Mabon headed inside, where Camille advanced, navigating in the dark until she used her staff to light the way.

The temperature changed from cool to warm, and the further they moved inside, the warmer it got. Perspiration covered their bodies. Camille untied the wrap around her shoulders and let it fall. The silk traveled over her thighs and landed in front of the prince.

"Make that the only garment you take off," Mabon said.

"I'm sure Tori wouldn't mind me putting the prince in some discomfort," she replied with a smirk.

"Galeno would mind."

She stopped and put her hand on his. "I'm flattered to be seen that way by your highness, but I assure you that my love will always be for my mate, as I know yours belongs to Tori's."

He nodded and tilted his head so they could proceed through the tunnel. Though they each had a mate and children of their own, something kept drawing him to her. The way she maneuvered her body at the slightest angle in the rock, the way her hair bounced on her shoulders and back, the way she smelled of a strong, sweet fragrance like the *Nicotiana* flower.

"Careful, my lord. These caverns seem to whisper desires neither one of us wants to execute." She stopped again.

"What is it?" he gulped.

"Aja."

Mabon listened but heard nothing; he only felt a wave of heat surge through his body. "What kind of beast is it?"

"I wanted to tell you earlier, my king," Camille replied with embarrassment. "To you, Aja will appear as a seductress."

"Don't tell me." Mabon held onto the wall; sweat trickled off his chin, and his stomach was in knots. "This only works on men."

"I'm sorry, your highness." She knit her eyebrows. "I can't stop it. I hope you're strong enough to control it."

Breathing heavily, Mabon formed a fist and brought his forehead to it. "Now it makes sense why you wanted an all-female squad." He blew out and closed his eyes. The pain in his joints stiffened him.

"Shall we?" Camille motioned to move further into the tunnel.

He opened his eyes and nodded again.

At this point, the air thickened and the walls grew hot. They had to be careful not to touch the surface as the heat singed their skin, which was a small price to pay for leaving behind his warriors, not to mention his family.

"Sada will awaken with Oda's wisdom, sire."

"That's not what worries me," he said through gritted teeth. "Sada has always been able to care for herself."

"Then it is the kingdom, for the twins are its future."

"It's more complicated than that." He bit his lip as a tight ball formed in his throat. The beast was calling his name. A melodic voice whispering in his ear. "King Waqar had this planned."

"I don't think he had planned for you to go after the book personally."

"It looked like the right thing to do."

As they neared a flickering light, they stopped and listened. Something was breathing heavily; its rhythm changed with each breath. Mabon looked in for the sleeping beast but saw a beautiful woman with long platinum blonde hair that covered her breasts, sitting inclined on a pearl the size of a boulder.

Yet Camille only saw the beast's head, twice the size of its body, with spikes traveling from the middle of its spine to its thick tail. It could be about ten feet tall on all fours. It had four eyes, and its feet were taloned. When it turned, drool fell off its jaws, and it licked its lips.

CHAPTER
16

Shadows rained on Yosemite; the air was thick and metallic gray. Rain wasn't in the forecast, but it arrived as another natural disaster befalling Earth. Only one thing stood in the way of the Avans dealing with the changes: the Garghons. Tamesis constructed a red barrier between them and the Avans, like a see-through wall. Quoba stepped back and had the warriors do the same.

"What are you playing at, witch?" he shouted as the clouds ran past them, pushing his feathers flat on his wings.

The Garghon witch raised her long arms, her matted hair stood up, and thunder ensued, bombarding the Avan side with lightning.

The warriors scattered out of the way of the bolts while the enemy laughed and snorted.

"*Cuidado*, Quoba," Gabriel said, securing the sword in his grasp. "She can hurt us all without the aid of that army she's got."

Quoba nodded and pinned an irritated look on the witch and her magic. "None of us have the kind of power you do. Let us wage a fair war with your army."

Tamesis lowered her arms, and her laugh echoed throughout the park like a sonic boom. "Earthquakes are splitting the land on each continent. Tsunamis claim thousands on the various shores, and you speak of fairness?" She laughed again. This time, her companions joined her by bashing each other's weapons against shields and rocks.

"Why don't you tell them?" a stout Garghon suggested. The Avans turned to each other, confused. Quoba watched their leader for an explanation.

Tamesis approached the wall and placed her blackened arms akimbo. Her eyes widened as her dry lips parted. "Give me the Avan with the high cheekbones and speckled white wings," she waved her arms, "and the natural disasters will stop."

The clouds continued rolling past them, chilling the air. A few drops fell like flakes, and Quoba searched for the Avan she described. More drops fell on his eyelashes, and he wiped them aside.

"No need to look further, friend," Edouard said. He stepped past some Avan sentinels, his short hair tussling in the wind. His sword was sheathed, and he dematerialized his shield.

"No!" Gabriel dropped his sword. It was mounted on its tip, inserted in the ground. The armor didn't shield him from the cold, and his teeth clattered. "You can't. We'll fight."

Edouard placed his hand on Gabriel's shoulder and shook his head. "If the catastrophes cease, then I must surrender to them."

"She wants to torture you." Gabriel lowered his gaze. "Nafuna had done the same to me." He pointed to the scars on his chest. "There has to be another way."

Quoba narrowed his eyes and took off his helmet. Sweat made its way from his scalp to the base of his neck, mixing with the rain. His wings pinched together. "Witch, you give your promise that the catastrophes on Earth will stop?"

"Of course," she said, grinning.

"The word of a Garghon isn't worth a thing!" one female Avan said.

"What will happen to the teacher?" asked another.

"Do they expect us to stay back while we hand over Edouard?" A blue-winged Avan held up his sword.

The Avans protested, and Quoba tried his best to reassure them of the pact. Though he didn't believe it himself, it was the only way to ensure the rest of the army didn't get hurt or killed. Would Galeno commend his efforts or condemn them? What would his prince do in moments like these?

Gabriel put his hand on the red wall Tamesis formed between them; the power emanating from it was high, and the scent of metal increased. "How will you keep your word, Tamesis?"

"Ah," she looked down at the human, "you call me by my name?"

"*¿Por qué no?*" Gabriel said, still shivering from the cold.

"I like that." Tamesis licked her lips. She raised her eyes to the sky and recited a few incoherent words. The sky cleared, and one could see the sun rise in the East. She turned back to the Avans and said, "The Garghons will throw down their weapons when the wall disappears. The Avan *teacher* will cross, and the spell will be lifted."

"But Tamesis, what about the king?" asked a Garghon who was missing a horn.

Tamesis's eyes darkened, and her entire body hardened, preventing her from twisting fast toward the speaker. "The king has what he wants."

The Garghons cheered for minutes and raised their weapons before throwing them down. The wall vanished along with the clanging sound of metal.

Edouard massaged his neck and gulped. He hoped Mabon had subdued the Garghon stronghold and he wouldn't have to suffer, but the idea was farfetched at best. If victory smiled on them, Tamesis hadn't shown any indication of its presence, and all he could hope for was mercy. He turned to Quoba and said, "Please care for Gabriel."

The commander's eyes watered as he nodded. He saluted the Avan and watched as the teacher crossed the partition linking both armies.

Garghons continued to drop their weapons, eyes boring down at him; some reached for his feathers and plucked a few out. He could hear Quoba stopping an Avan from attacking and the witch's chortle as Edouard fell to his knees. The heat intensified the further into the Garghon army he strode. Tamesis flew up and landed in front of Edouard, took hold of his shoulders, and slashed off the strap to his chest plate. Exercising her magic, she bonded him with chains.

Edouard tried to break free, but the more he pulled, the tighter the chains became.

Tamesis grabbed his jaw and moved him sideways. "Now, my pet, you will pay for what you did." She hovered above the army, holding Edouard with the claws on her bare feet, and addressed Quoba, "Remember our bargain!" And she tossed the teacher to the Garghons.

Before any of the Avans could charge toward them, the Garghons flew off without their weapons. Only the witch's laughter careened over them.

"What are we going to do?" a thin Avan asked.

"The Garghons will break their promise," said another with a husky voice.

"And surely break Edouard!" a few alleged.

"We can't let Edouard be a prisoner." Gabriel took off his helmet.

"The Garghons toy with lives, my friend." Quoba picked up his helmet, placed it back on, and faced his army. "We must make sure Earth is safe from catastrophes and aid those in need."

"Wait," Gabriel said as he got in front of the large Avan, "what about Edouard?"

"Yes!" said another Avan. "We can't leave him to fend off a whole defense force."

Quoba looked down. He wanted to reassure the young

man that it wouldn't be the last time they'd see Edouard or that he wasn't a coward for letting this happen. He wanted to follow and hunt the witch personally for having begrudgingly hurt the Rosales brothers. But he couldn't. He must contain his anger and think of the whole. He raised his eyes and formed a fist.

"We have to get going."

CHAPTER 17

Outside the Avan castle, the clatter of the enemy's flapping wings increased. Their screeching coiled the ears, intensifying their due arrival on Ava. Galeno had his two elite guards sound the alarm and get more sentries to protect the castle. Already, he noticed the Garghons frightening the few commoners below. Most have gone into shelter by now, which is best at the moment, but if the need arose for more arms, he would call for them.

"Your highness, let's get you to safety," Galeno said as he turned away from the window and sheathed his sword. Luckily, the twins should be safe with Tori and Urmi in the next room since the walls were two feet thick.

Still holding Oda's amulet in her hand, Queen Kalani tipped the bowl Willa brought over, and the water sparkled like a clear blue lake until the image of her son, Mabon, appeared. She gasped, toppled the bowl, and fell on her knees.

"My queen!" Willa slid over the water and assisted the queen to her feet.

"Death to Avans!"

"Whatever it is you saw, your highness, it would have to wait." Galeno heard the Garghon battle cry again. He removed his sword and materialized his shield. His muscles tensed as he took on a fighting stance.

A Garghon broke through the glass window and landed in front of the Avan. It balanced two clubs of different sizes. One had spikes attached to the tip, and the other had been cut but not sanded.

"You must come with us," the creature addressed the queen, but kept his beady yellow eyes fixed on Galeno.

"Not likely, dung breath." Galeno cut off part of the creature's club and jabbed it with his elbow.

The Garghon raised his clubs and attacked Galeno, striking his shield repeatedly.

The force made Galeno's arm sore, but he was used to battle wounds and the pain that accompanied them. When he noticed the creature raise his clubs again, he bent one knee, manipulated his sword below his shield, and struck the Garghon's ankles. He sliced open skin, and strange dark blood dripped onto his sword.

The Garghon bounced back with a squeal. "You will pay."

Galeno maneuvered away from the creature's clubs, and said, "But if you can't afford the charge..."

The creature dropped the clubs and ran toward the Avan, pushing him against the wall, winding him, and pressing the shield on his arm. The jolt left deep red welts on Galeno's forearm, and the weight of his adversary pressed on his ribs. He used his foot to squeeze between him and the Garghon, then, sliding his foot further, he pulled the Garghon's ankle.

The creature fell back on the floor, hitting his head.

As a boy, Galeno excelled at sports, academics, and anything put before him. Galeno grinned and pushed his opponent back. Today, he excelled at annoying his opponent by knocking him down over and over. Garghons were on Avan ground, and he had a weak queen and heirs to the throne he must protect. He held his sword in one hand and secured his shield in the other, but before he could pursue the assault, another Garghon entered through the window, then another, each taking hold of Willa and the Queen, who had managed to remain by Sada's side to incubate the princess lest Oda's spirit cease to connect with hers.

"Galeno, the warrior," the last creature said with a smack to his lips as he crawled his way in, his wing tips sharp as nails. He stood by the crumbled window frame of the room with more than a dozen soldiers.

Galeno replied with a tilt of his head. "And the one who would cut off your head."

The Garghons stepped closer and showed their misshapen teeth.

"Baqir is who you address, Avan scum!" He raised his axe and brought it down on Galeno's sword. Metal clashed and clanged, forming sparks.

An Avan squad of ten arrived and met the Garghons face-to-face to battle each other without further delay. The creatures screamed and cried their battle song, smashing their heads and weapons against their enemy. Galeno watched a trusted warrior fall on his sword; another was pierced across the chest; and others were bleeding at various places, making the room fill with the scent of iron and sweat. The Garghons didn't fare any better, but the odds were not even. Galeno knew that. The Avan army was thin. The commoners on Ava would have to pick up a sword if this war was to be in their favor.

Two Garghons made their way to Queen Kalani again. She had returned to shielding Sada with a mystical spell, forming a cloak. Her flushed face told Galeno that the strain was getting too heavy. His Queen, who once battled alongside the warriors, leading them to victory, was now withering before their eyes. Prince Mabon had become the new hope, and he couldn't have returned at such an appalling time.

Baqir used his talons to scratch Galeno on his biceps.

Galeno backed away and sensed the pain grating its way into his skin. He raised his eyes and narrowed them.

Baqir grinned and swung his sword, but Galeno headbutted

the Garghon leader, catching him off guard. Baqir growled.

Pushing him down, Galeno ran after the two creatures who went for the queen.

Baqir hoisted himself up after the Avan. "You're as quick as your tongue, which *I'll* cut out!"

Galeno turned to face Baqir when the queen let go of the cloak surrounding Sada and elevated herself high toward the ceiling. A bright light emanated from behind her, enlarging her glittery wings.

"Hear me." Her pale lips trembled.

Willa picked up a fallen sword and got in front of Sada's body.

"Why should we?" a Garghon asked, his club around an Avan's throat.

Queen Kalani rolled up her sleeves, and her forearms changed to a golden hue. She sent a bolt of lightning at the creature, causing his body to convulse and burn.

The two Garghons who tried getting close to the queen backed away. Their faces were skewed under her shadow.

Baqir wiped his mouth with the back of his hand and spat dark blood on the ground.

"Your majesty, it's better to stand down or your nestlings will be hurt." He raised his splintered sword and pointed to the deformed Jaime Rosales by the broken doorway.

Jaime held the twins under his armpits; his chin had lengthened, and two small horns sat atop his head, but it was his tortured eyes that marked him as the puppet the Garghons expected of Avans.

Galeno had never seen a man turn into a creature so vile. Whoever this man was, his eyes were glazed and his lips turned. The deformed man carried both twins with him, dangling them from his shoulders like a brute. How did he come by them? That's a question for another time. If Galeno were to attack or move forward, the twins would surely get hurt, but he needed to try. He looked up at the queen; she shook her head, and her saddened eyes watered as she descended.

Galeno cursed, then gave the order for his army to lower their weapons. He threw his on the ground and watched as the queen came down and met Baqir.

"Speak your terms, Garghon," she said.

"Oh, King Waqar has made it plain and clear that you should visit him at the fort to serve your last days for murdering our queen." His eyes twinkled.

"Ridiculous!" Galeno expressed himself, placing his injured arm on his sword.

Queen Kalani silenced her elite commander with a penetrating look. "Surely, there must be a trade-off to these terms?"

With a wry smile, Baqir said, "Not really, Queen."

Romeo ran past the Garghons and between the Avans, causing havoc. He nipped at heels and bit calves. Garghons stepped out of the way, and a few tried to strike the menacing animal as the dog made its way to the twins. When Romeo reached Baqir, he stopped and spread his front legs; his hackles rose, and he bared his teeth. Saliva dripped from his mouth, and the once-loving dog appeared determined to bite the Garghon or die trying.

"What is this?" Baqir asked, amused. "This Avan beast wants to do away with us, but we have the upper hand."

Queen Kalani calmed the dog by covering him in a cooling mist and having him retreat.

The Garghons laughed at Romeo's retreat and began picking up the Avans' weapons.

"Don't do that," a voice said.

Tori stood by the doorway with Urmi, her distraught face flushed as she held back the tears.

"You're a Human. What can you do?" Baqir asked.

"Plenty." She opened a bag filled with pellets and had Urmi whisper a magical spell into it. Then Tori threw the pellets at the Garghons. Each small object hit their bodies and exploded with enough force to stun them.

The Avans grabbed their weapons and attacked the dazed enemy.

Realizing the dog no longer remained idle and the sudden change of events, Baqir secured Jaime and the twins he carried and gave the signal for his army to retreat.

CHAPTER
18

King Waqar sat on his throne, his hand under his chin, the other caressing the image of a scowling Garghon head on the arm rest. He watched his warriors through a magic window that spun white around the edges in the middle of the cavern, making it the only light emanating. The vents where the lava used to flow in this cavern were dark oases like the old magma chamber below, where they used to hang intruders. His grin showed the sharp teeth, and he moved his hand away from his chin. The king's dark skin seemed to protrude from the rock surface like a carved statue.

The plans to secure the twins had worked, and the Avans were down a would-be king for his stupidity. The Earth had enough devastation wreaked upon it that humans would suffer and struggle for years. Soon, the island would be sprawled with dead Avans. The Garghons would select the best of the warriors to alter into more Garghons.

In the distant cave opening, King Waqar noticed Tamesis make her way through the darkened alternative path away from the battle outside. She left half her squad fighting while the rest followed her with an Avan slave she had procured.

She stopped in front of the king, raised her charred wings, and bowed.

"Oh, mighty one, we were glorious in our battle with the

Avans on Earth." She raised her yellowed eyes and met the king's.

Waqar lifted his long, bent talon. "Who is that?"

With his chin up, the Avan said, "I am Edouard."

"Insolent dog!" A Garghon soldier used his hammer and hit the Avan in the stomach.

Tamesis went to Edouard, grabbed his hair, and pushed his head back. "This belongs to me," she hissed. She glanced back at the king. "It owes me for interfering with the human brothers."

King Waqar raised his eyebrows and rubbed his chin. "What about Earth? Why have the floods and other catastrophes stopped?"

Tamesis released Edouard's hair and straightened her dark wings. She screwed up her eyes and looked around at the soldiers.

"There was no need to do further work on Earth, your most high." She tightened her grip on the hilt of her sword. "The connection I have with the human called Jaime told me the twins were on their way."

"So, you took it upon yourself to stop the darkness consuming Earth?"

"We have what we want." She uncurled her talons, then closed her fist, extending her arm toward the Garghon king. "Earth is but a speck in our plans. What good would it do us if the people were gone? Without the power the royal family wields, we can take any planet whenever we want."

"You make a good point, Tamesis." King Waqar nodded, and his horn tips fizzled.

"Of course," Tamesis paced, "if your liege wants us to return to Earth..."

"No need." He pounded the armrest. "It's best you be here to complete the boy's transformation."

Edouard raised his eyebrow.

King Waqar stood, his bottom half covered in leather, and

his wings folded together. Then they opened wide. Their angular edges and alula were without a thumb, only something pointed like a nail. "However, you have an Avan warrior."

"Actually, I'm a teacher first," Edouard said, using his chained hands to point to himself.

A Garghon was going to strike the Avan, but the king stopped him with a wave of his arm. Bending to gaze upon the Avan, the king smelled the salty sweat on his body and the fear he harbored under the courage he foolishly used. "Then you won't mind helping me with a lesson."

Tamesis widened her eyes. "Your highness!"

"Of course." Edouard backed away from the king's hot, spicy breath, and licked his dry bottom lip. "I'm not a sorcerer. I utilize the limited magic we Avans are given from birth."

"Tamesis has disobeyed her orders." King Waqar approached him, and his wide shoulders blocked his throne.

"And you want to use me as an example?"

The king snorted on top of the Avan and stood tall. The height of the Garghon made Edouard wince.

The king gestured, and the Garghons formed two lines. They faced each other, and Edouard was at the head.

Edouard gulped, but didn't lose his composure.

"If you survive the lesson, Tamesis will keep you as her slave, to do with as she pleases."

Tamesis let go of her sword; her chest tightened, and she bared her teeth.

"If you don't," King Waqar snarled, "we can assume you weren't a good teacher."

Baqir heard the last words King Waqar spoke as he returned to the Garghon stronghold. He found an Avan tortured within the line of negligence. He shivered at the thought, for many didn't survive, and all for not doing what they were told. He smiled as he neared the king's throne—the sound of flesh ripping.

"Ah, Baqir, you have the twins?" King Waqar asked without

losing sight of the way his Garghons beat on the Avan teacher. Some of his feathers were plucked, his leg burned, and his arms injured. Yet he hadn't fallen or stopped striking back, which was commendable.

Bowing, Baqir said, "The Human is holding the twin hostages below." He swayed his eyes to the left and noticed Tamesis beside King Waqar, her crimson stare wading across toward the Avan, licking her lips each time blood splattered from his mouth. What they wanted from the Avan was beyond Baqir, but all *he* wanted was to be rewarded for bringing the twins to the stronghold.

"Do you wish to see the brats, mighty one?"

"Take them to the Doom Room to await their destiny with death. Secure it and make sure the battle outside is in our favor," Waqar pronounced.

"Of course," Baqir replied, bowing and keeping his eye toward the Avan, who stumbled to the end of the line.

"Don't let them out of your sight until you secure them, Baqir. You didn't bring them all this way to let me down."

Baqir nodded and saluted with his club, then made his way to the prisoners.

Turning his attention back to the line, King Waqar clapped, and the Garghons moved away from their formation to allow him passage. "Very formidable, teacher. You have saved your captor and sealed your fate."

Edouard took deep breaths and wiped his mouth. His left eye was sealed shut, sweat and dirt made their way to the injury, and he squinted repeatedly. He massaged his abdomen, which already showed signs of bruising.

"I'm glad... my performance," Edouard blew out air and continued with a hoarse voice, "was entertaining, but don't you think... Avans will be at your door soon?"

"Impudent pest!" the Garghon King waved his hand, and fire blew out of a hole behind the warriors. They crouched but resumed their stance. He took the Avan by his wing, dangling him off the ground.

Edouard grimaced as a charging ping crawled to his shoulder blades.

"Get him out of my sight, Tamesis, and make sure the book is safe."

"Oh, about that book..." Edouard raised his finger and said, "it doesn't belong to you."

King Waqar shook the Avan and threw him down with such force that Edouard let out a deep grunt. His body trembled at the king's feet.

Tamesis collected the Avan and said, "Yes, your most high, the book shall be our victory, and I will make sure this one pays the price most dearly."

Dragging Edouard through another vent in the rock wall, Tamesis watched as Baqir flew out with the warriors to finish the fight outside, while King Waqar continued to the Doom Room with one of his servants.

Dumping Edouard inside a dark room, Tamesis lit it with the flip of a stick outside the entrance.

Edouard crawled aside and took hold of the slippery rock wall. His fingers numbed at the cold texture, and his breathing became more rapid and laborious. He placed his other hand over his left eye and turned toward the witch, who stepped closer to him in the cell.

"Is there more you want from me?"

She grabbed hold of the teacher's hair and pulled it back.

Edouard gritted his teeth and felt the sting of pain all over his body, especially the burn on his right leg that had dried blood stuck to his torn pants.

"Yes, I desire more from you." She let go of his hair and smoothed the sweat around his bare shoulders.

Edouard raised his right eyebrow, and his ribs rose up and down. "You're not... thinking of killing me so soon?"

Tamesis grinned; her flat lips stretched to the point where a single tooth stuck out, and her eyes flickered bright orange. "I have plans for you. If the transformation is successful with the boy, I may use you for another experiment."

He let his head fall against the wall, letting his wings cushion his back. "You want... you want to transform me into a Garghon?"

"You catch on fast, Avan."

"What for?" He let out a breath. "Is there a problem with the male community here?"

Tamesis raised her hand and slashed Edouard across the chest.

He fell forward, hands trembling, and watched as the blood dripped from the corner of the wound.

"You're mine!"

Edouard's chest tightened, which didn't help the damage, and he slumped down on the wall until he sat on the ground. His right leg was all purple from the Garghon blows. It was a miracle he still lived. At least he had Mabon to thank for helping train him. Then he recalled the way the witch saw his ordeal; her eyes almost watered, and she seemed to take it as an insult that *she* wasn't the one executing the harm. He had to try to get out of her insane clutches.

"I have no more time for this," she said, licking his blood off her hand with her tongue. "I'll return to finish what was started, pretty mess. The book must be safe."

"I thought it was already safe?"

"Hah! That army outside led them straight to it. Some Avans have breached the premises, and it's up to me to destroy them."

"Really?"

Tamesis took hold of his jaw; her talons gently curled around his face. "Yes, pretty mess, I will return." And she rubbed her sandpaper cheek against his before departing.

The sizzling static sparked along the frame of the entrance, and an electrical barrier appeared, sealing the cell, as the witch stepped out of the room, which was fine with Edouard. He was tired, hurt, and scared for his life, but even more so for Mabon's children. Where would Ava be without the royals?

CHAPTER 19

Mabon's knees buckled. His hands hit the gravel to stop the impact. Sweat dripped off his face in large droplets, and his insides tightened. He missed his family. He missed watching the moon's light set on Ava.

Pain shot through his groin, and he made fists, collecting the dirt with his fingers. The cavern walls seemed to close in on him, and he covered his face.

"What you see is not what you think, my prince," Camille said. She knelt beside him. She wanted to soothe his anguish with a small caress, but that would invite trouble. Instead, she turned to the beast on the rock, caught sight of its amulet around its neck, and muttered a sequence of incantations. She rose and pressed her index finger against her thumb. A small spark ignited, growing into a blue whirlwind. She approached Aja, ready to throw sparks at it, when the beast started to sing.

Aja's song broke past her spell and reached Mabon. He curved his back; his wings smacked against the top of the tunnel, and a few rocks tumbled down on them. With a quick flick of her wrists, Camille conjured a forcefield and blocked the rocks. Pulling her sleeves up, she waved her hands in front of her, forming a rainbow-like circle that glittered with twinkling stars.

The beast tilted its head, then turned it around like an owl.

It thumped its tail and made a strange sound vibrating within the walls. Curious, it approached Camille, but as it did, Mabon convulsed on the ground.

"Make it stop!" He turned over and hit his elbow on a boulder. His tanned body was covered in dust. He tried to use his own magic to stop Aja, but all he managed was to feel his forearms burn as if he had taken a drug.

Closing her eyes, Camille proceeded to draw the beast toward her, waving her arms wider and making the circle larger. She sensed the amulet was the source of Aja's power, and she musically hummed a spell to lure the beast.

The beast curled its tail and drooled, clawing the air as it reached for the rainbow in front of the Avan.

Realizing the beast could not speak but only conjure songs to force men to grovel at its feet, Camille spread her arms wide and closed them in front of her to fling the circle on top of Aja.

The minute Aja touched the rainbow, it turned into a strong net from which it could not break free. No matter how hard it pushed and pulled with its talons, the net smothered her. Aja made a deafening cry and spat onto the net, making it sizzle.

Dropping her fatigued arms, Camille knelt beside the prince, taking deep breaths. She watched him shudder uncontrollably. He was weakened but fighting. She admired that about him. Galeno had said half-breeds would not reach Avan's capacity, but she scoffed at the idea. The prince had enough strength to hold on. She placed her hands on his broad shoulders, pushing him down to settle him, but he wouldn't stop. His jolting movements sent Camille back against the wall, bumping her head into it.

Incense trailed a smoky line toward Mabon. Camille turned to the beast, and its skin fell off, melting onto the ground like candle wax, followed by a bright moon glow. The acrid smell of rotten flesh jarred Camille, but what awed her was what came out of the large beast's body: a beautiful woman whose naked skin rivaled a young virgin's.

Without moving its lips, Aja said, "You dare trespass." Her silver-blonde hair flowed back, and she stepped closer to Mabon's body. With the trembling over, he was now breathing heavily.

"Leave him," Camille demanded. She hoisted herself off the ground, striking the beast with magical darts.

They struck Aja's skin, but soon it healed. She formed a sleek smile with those dusty rose lips.

"You want the Dark Magic Book?"

"If possible." Camille took her fighting stance and wished she had worn the battle clothes Galeno had set for her instead of her sorceress garb. "But we don't have to fight."

Pointing to the prince's body, Aja said, "I want the male." Levitating him toward her, Aja set him at her feet and removed his armor, leaving the pants unbuttoned.

"Stop!"

"You dare!" Aja's silver eyes turned into dark pools of ink.

"I will not exchange my future king for a book or turn him into your plaything."

"So, this is a king?" Aja traced Mabon's chest with her fingers, causing him to moan.

"Great Aja," Camille let out a controlled shriek, "help us and stop the Garghons from unleashing the dark magic in the book. They are only using you to destroy Earth and find a way to control Ava."

The beast raised her arms, and a strong wind formed behind her. "Because I'd rather have what's under my feet!" And she summoned the wind to slam into Camille.

Camille hit the wall with such force that her shoulder blades pressed into the rock, scraping her skin. The beast was strong, but she knew the amulet would inhibit her powers. Maybe sealing her in the amulet would detain her. The force continued to press on Camille's back, causing her to reel in pain.

Mabon saw what Aja was doing to Camille, and he sat up. His ribs squeezed, making it hard to keep up. He raised his hand and concentrated on a loose rock above the beast. Blood dripped from his nose, and he made a fist, quickly bringing his arm down. The rock came down on top of Aja, stopping her from flattening Camille into the rock wall but making her angrier.

Aja rose, arms at her side; her hair flowed like tentacles, her silver eyes darkened, and her skin shimmered like sand crystals. Fire streamed from her fingers, adding to the heat already in the tight cavern.

At the same time, the wall parted open behind the prince, where the lava flowed, and a Garghon stepped through.

Camille inhaled the dampness and rubbed her shoulder. "You?"

Tamesis lifted her club and the room lit up. Her nose scrunched at the sight of the beast.

"What have you done?"

CHAPTER 20

Dawn arrived on Earth, and the moon had retreated further from Ava. The last moon strands left Sada's fingers. The stars hid behind the sky like children playing hide-and-seek. Violent gales remained on Earth as the magic upon it diminished volcanic activity, hurricanes, and other catastrophes. The people who had courage did much to help, and those without learned to have courage in the midst of the chaos they had never seen before, calling it 'Armageddon' or an 'Apocalypse.' The Avans distributed themselves among the people to better aid them. Similar turmoil ensued on Ava after the Garghons attacked. Avans banded together to protect the castle, and others sought shelter.

Sada sensed all this from her bed as the wizard's power flowed through the river of life in her body. She sensed the hearts of those around her, and tears flowed from her closed eyes—pain and suffering; hurt and sadness; hope and despair. Her throat ached, and she heard a familiar voice in her head say:

"Daughter of Mabon, you have the heart of a warrior. You have excelled in the arts and have made both Camille and I proud with your abilities. Take these additional powers and protect what's important."

"Oda?" Sada whispered.

"She's awake!" she heard Willa call out.

"Good," the queen said. She picked up a cloth beside a glass bowl of water and dipped it before squeezing the excess with one hand.

"How is that good, your highness?" Willa's voice cracked. "We have lost much."

"Sada's power is magnified for the task ahead." She went to her granddaughter and placed the warm cloth on her forehead.

The water trickled down her temples and moistened her scalp. Oda's voice echoed in her head. Were they words left over from her trance? Or was Oda linked to her until she could master everything he knew? The condition was novel, and the task set. Even as a child in school, she could understand magic without studying it. There was one other student Oda thought would best her: Declan, but he was shy and kept his thoughts well hidden.

Sada opened her eyes and smiled uneasily. "I'm sorry I wasn't there to stop the twins from being taken."

"How did she know?" Willa asked, bringing drinking water and some biscuits from the far table.

"Sada had always been able to read thoughts." Queen Kalani turned the cloth over. "Now, it includes the ability to read the universe. Though she won't be able to understand everything, with Oda's guidance, her focus will be better." She placed her hand over Sada's and squeezed it.

Returning the gesture, Sada sat up slowly, letting the cloth fall onto her lap.

"Forgive me, my royals, but are we safe?"

"Safety is a temporary thing." Sada drank the water. "It is better to have hope for an existence without war."

"Oda has passed on his magical essence to you, child." Queen Kalani brushed her granddaughter's loose hair back. "You are an Avan Sorceress, and I should not refer to you as a child anymore."

She hugged the queen, and after the embrace, she asked, "When are we going after them?"

"Galeno has the guards in place around Ava. Tori assists the Avans in preparing for a second attack." The queen looked away; her voice almost faint. "Your father is in danger as we speak. Camille is with him, but she needs your help. Not even her magic can contain two witches."

"What do you mean?"

"The Garghons have utilized the book to bring about a beast from what little Camille was able to send as word." Queen Kalani stood and led Sada to the tipped-over basin. "Look for yourself, and you will see what you need to know to help your father."

Sada set the drinking glass down and looked into the water. Flashes of light and ripples formed a rainbow pattern. Once they cleared, her breath left her, and she held onto the edge of the table to steady herself. This was new to her. Oda's magic was above everyone's, and they dealt with ancient spells. She could only tap so much without convulsing; her body was rigid from the strain of holding on.

The scent of wet, moldy rock filled the air; her head ached, and blood dripped from her right nostril, landing in the water. The blood spread like paint washed down the stream, and she could see her father. Hurt. Anguish. Suffering. Damaged. Her body tensed. She spotted Camille blocking something she could not make out, and then her mentor was thrust against the wall.

Sada's body rocked. "I cannot see…"

Covering her mouth, Willa gasped.

"Concentrate," Queen Kalani said.

Sada narrowed her eyes, and she gripped the table tighter. Her fingernails scratched the bottom of the wood. The pain pulsing in her head hammered louder, and both her nostrils bled into the basin, causing the water to thicken. This time, she saw the beast—its two forms like a Joker's costume—on a card she saw in Oda's bookcase. Her oversized body held up a round, crinkly head. Fangs and two horns adorned her head. She noticed the amulet it wore in neon light and the book within its eye. Sada's hands slipped off the table, and Willa caught her from behind.

"Princess!"

Galeno had sent a herald to Earth and informed Quoba of what transpired on Ava. He ordered Quoba's team to join Mabon's forces and apprehend the Garghons. The people of Earth were in good hands with their heroes, and the Avans had done their part to make sure the Garghons had been driven out. Humans had a right to their stories without the Avans getting referred to in their legends. All of them could mask their wings and strength. Their armor was gone, and the clothes humans wore covered their bodies, but Quoba knew they were from different worlds. Their speech was different, as Gabriel and Tori could attest.

Only Avans could hear the magic horn attached to Quoba's belt. He summoned them to convene at a desolate location. Removing the eight-inch horn from his lips, he turned to Gabriel, who had climbed onto the rubble of a house laden with trees after a tropical cyclone hit Australia. The Garghons used the Dark Magic Book to cause this oddity.

"We are called back, my friend," Quoba said.

"That explains the noiseless horn."

Gabriel wanted to return to the world above, see Sada, and tell her how he felt one last time. Maybe she would forgive the things he last said, but he couldn't get Edouard out of his head. The Garghons were going to kill him.

"Duty calls, Gabriel," Quoba pronounced, patting him on the back. "As the only one without wings, I want you to stay close to your team."

"You think Edouard will be—"

"He will."

Gabriel nodded but thought of the other Avans fighting the Garghons. "Why didn't Galeno mention anything about the prince?"

"There are too many details, and a message cannot convey them all."

His voice trailed off as his well-rounded shoulders slumped forward. Quoba knew well what war could do. No one was immune to its pull toward death. Turning to the Avan force, Quoba divulged, "There's no time to waste. The young princes have been taken, and we must fly to the Garghon stronghold without rest."

The news hit Gabriel like a ten-foot wave. His brother was sent to a safe room in the castle with the princes after the ordeal with Tamesis. What became of him? His eyes were filled with dread.

Creasing his brow, Quoba said, "I know not of your brother."

"I haven't been honest with Jaime."

"Then, next time you meet, you should try."

The Avans converted their clothes into armor and materialized their wings. The sun behind them was a fiery ball, glowing intensely. The heat bore down on their skin, making it tight.

Sweat dripped from Gabriel's temples. Dirt stuck to it as the wind blew past him. Then, two Avans grabbed him and flew up.

CHAPTER
21

Jaime looked at his hands with disgust. They had darkened and thinned as his fingers elongated. Fangs hung over his lower lip, and on the top of his head were two horns, small and pointy like a devil costume he'd seen children wear on his least favorite holiday, Halloween. His eyesight changed, as well. Where green and blue colors soothed, now brightened. While red and brown shades darkened, now flickered at odd moments.

"Do you think he knows who he is?" asked Xio.

Xander squeezed his arm against the cold of the large room, empty and filled with the echoes of past torture. Other creatures have gone through torture to give King Waqar what he wanted. His head's pounding increased as the experiences he sensed in the room made him wince. Finally, he answered, "He knows."

"Don't do that," Xio said.

"Do what?" Xander let his arm fall.

"The cryptic thing." Xio raised his fingers and made hanging quotes.

"And you?" Xander pointed to his brother's back, where two stumps protruded out from under his shirt. "Those things didn't shrink."

Xio looked away and stuffed his fists in his pocket. He

knew what the Garghons wanted with him. Worse, he knew what they did to him. If his mother found out, she would freak. What if his father knew?

"They want to use all of us," Jaime managed to say. He wobbled toward the twins. His face twisted in the dimly lit room. "It's all my fault."

"So, what's new?" Xio hung his head and kicked a pebble.

"We have to get out of here," Jaime said, exasperated.

"Good idea, genius," Xio said. "But there are no doors in this place."

"I can find the door." Xander sat on the ground and placed his hands on his lap, breathing slowly. But before he could start, Xio fell to his knees, groaning.

"What is it?"

Xio moved his arm, gesturing to Xander. His stomach burned like acid does when coming into contact with skin. He continued to writhe in pain, and he felt the stubs on his back start to push out. A tiny tornado formed in the corner of the room.

"Make him stop!" Jaime pulled Xander's shirt off as he lifted him, then leaned down. "Or I will."

"No!" The boy slapped his arm, and Jaime cringed back.

Xio fell to his side, and the whites of his eyes turned black. The tornado grew another inch.

Stepping closer to the twin, Jaime shook Xio, trying to break the boy's trance.

Xander used his telekinesis to shove Jaime against the rock wall, then turned his attention to his brother by forming a sparkling blue-green sphere with clear waves like a marble. He tossed it to Xio, and the sphere penetrated his back to hold the stumps in place and protect him.

Squirming on the ground, Xio kicked the dirt with his heels. He didn't want this change to happen. He wouldn't be able to face his family, but the pressure was too great. A black liquid from under his fingernails leaked out, covering his skin.

Xio could barely see his hands. The liquid had blackened them like a bird swimming out of an oil spill.

A growing halo orbited Xander, touching the ceiling. Xander focused on his brother, and the light flickered, ready to strike.

Jaime covered his sensitive eyes from the spotlight. Turning, a wall opened behind him, and in stepped King Waqar with his servant.

"So, it begins," he said.

"Never!" Xander brought down the light hitting the ceiling onto the tornado, drawing it swiftly to the Garghon King.

In turn, the king formed a horned shield with elaborately carved spirals, blocking the boy's attack. "Not bad, mutt."

Coming down, Xander headed to his brother, who continued to roll on the ground. His arms were black, and the stubs on his back tore through the shirt, revealing tiny wings. Xander felt a twitch on his own back.

"Of course," the king commented as he knelt over Xio. "Your brother will have to go through his transformation, too."

Squinting from the stubs pushing out, tears streamed down Xio's blackened face.

"You will not take my brother," he said gruffly.

Xander raised himself and motioned his hands in front of him, placing them in front of his heart. He formed a small blue sphere and looked up at the king.

King Waqar stood and watched as the boy created the sphere and wondered how the light surrounding his half-human body varied from yellow to green and what a mere boy could accomplish with little knowledge of magic.

"I know it can be reversed," Xander said as he made the sphere solid.

"Not after the spell is complete." King Waqar's breath grew hot and drifted out from between his lips.

"I won't let it happen." Xander threw the sphere onto the Garghon King's chest.

King Waqar fell back from the unexpected weight. His eyes darkened, and he blew his breath toward the boy. The steam singed Xander and made him tumble back.

The Garghon servant clapped while Xio's anguished cry echoed in the Doom Room as he watched his brother fall.

"Look, great one," said the servant. "If you hurt one, the other hurts, too."

"I can see that, fool," King Waqar said as he glanced down at his chest. The sphere attack left a mark on his skin that he didn't expect. "This one is powerful as a boy. Imagine what he would be able to do as a man?"

He waved his arm and pulled Jaime away from the wall. "Take hold of him!"

At first, Jaime resisted the king's pull, but the more he did, the more his face jittered and his legs bent toward Xander.

Shaking his head, Xander rubbed his right eye before catching the Garghon's stare. With a fixed stare and scowl, Xander raised his hand to attack, but Jaime took hold of his arm from behind.

"What are you doing?" Xander pushed Jaime, but he rammed himself against the boy, winding him.

"Don't fight any more," Jaime said through clenched teeth.

Xander rubbed his aching stomach. Gabriel's brother was under Garghon control. There were too many to fight, and he already felt the pulsing sting in his head increase. His ability to call upon the locket's power decreased, and Queen Kalani's surge was almost depleted. He needed rest as much as he needed to get his brother to safety. There was no telling what they would become once their wings grew out. But he couldn't allow the Garghons to use him, not after what happened years ago. Caution was better suited when dealing with the Garghons, as his father taught repeatedly. Jaime grabbed hold of Xander's arms and held him tight.

"Unfortunately, you must live in order for my weapon to live." The Garghon King picked Xio up, and the boy's body became limp.

"Let him go!" Xander levitated Jaime out of the way and knocked the servant to the ground. His breathing was ragged now, and sweat dripped from his forehead.

King Waqar curled his fingers around Xio.

"Stop!" Xander reached for his brother.

"Now that I have your attention, son of Ava," King Waqar said, "kneel before me."

Xander shook his head, but when the king curled his fingers further, he complied.

"Good," King Waqar said with a grin. "Let the chains, which will wrap themselves around you, keep you from Xio's destiny."

Xander took a deep breath and watched as chains formed on the rock walls and crawled out, snaking their way to him. They wrapped around his ankles, legs, arms, and neck, choking him before sending him an electric shock.

CHAPTER
22

Sada watched the ripples from the pool of water in a bowl settle on the floor of the queen's study. The water's surface showed her father, his face scrunched up in pain, and the veins on his arms bulging. Hot. Cold. A tingle made her fingers move, and she spotted Camille sprawled on the floor after some rays hit her before the water completely cleared.

"Princess?" Willa's voice cracked. Her trembling hand waved over Sada's glazed and fixed eyes.

Queen Kalani placed her hand on her granddaughter's shoulder. "Your father is in great danger. His body cannot withstand this much pressure."

Blinking, Sada heard the nervous pacing of someone who had entered through the unhinged double doors. She turned and spotted Tori with Romeo. Sada lowered her eyes to her hands and brought them to cleanse the blood from her nose until Willa gave her the cloth to wipe the excess off. "There isn't much time, your highness."

Tori stopped pacing and stood next to Willa, who was at least four inches taller. She spotted the bowl and asked, "Did you see the twins?"

"The twins..." Sada brought her hand to her chest, feeling her heart beat to the rhythm of her brothers, who were undergoing their own trial. "They aren't in danger yet," Sada finally said. Though she lied, she couldn't tell them what she knew. Everything seemed so distant and unreal. She couldn't tell her family of the damage the Garghons planned on the twins. She watched Tori's face wrinkle with worry, and she said in a reassuring voice, "They will fend for themselves until Prince Mabon can get to them."

"If you haven't noticed, Mabon isn't here. He's busy getting folded into—"

"Tori!" Queen Kalani's voice echoed in the room. "We understand your concern, but your husband is in peril and must be freed. Galeno is working on a plan to help get them back." The queen stood and took hold of Tori's hands, and her voice softened. "We will get all of them back. Is everyone ready?"

Tori nodded and lowered her eyes, ashamed of her outburst. "I'm sorry, but my family's in jeopardy, and there's nothing I can do with forces beyond my control."

The queen sighed and squeezed Tori's hand.

Romeo tapped Tori with his nose, and she looked down at him. His glossy eyes were a window of confidence.

The queen let go of Tori and turned back to Sada. "What do you plan?"

"You know what I must do, your highness." Sada rose and spread her wings, stretching the feathers and cracking her neck. She had been in a trance for too long. "A transference must be done."

"Transference? What's that?" Tori wrapped her arms around herself, not liking what the word might mean for Avans.

"Such a spell hasn't been used for two decades. The repercussions might be dire."

"My queen," Sada bowed, "dire is what this war has become."

"I cannot allow such a spell. What if the damage worsens this war?"

"Please," Tori lowered her arms and faced the young Avan. She saw Mabon's determined stare—a world in each eye that told of suffering and hope. "What is this transference? Please tell me what you plan."

Sada paused and took a deep breath. When she met Tori on the farm, she found her emotional and strong-minded. A strange combination, but she was Human like Gabriel, and humans did not have the kind of restraint Avans did until she realized they weren't much different. "I must switch places with my father."

The words sank into Tori's stomach like regurgitated bile. "But that means you'll deal with whatever caused Mabon's pain."

Sada turned away and stood by the doorway.

Tori continued, "The Garghons will torture you!"

"If that's what it takes to secure the Dark Magic Book and bring my father home..." Her voice trailed off, and Sada flew out of the room toward the courtyard. Three sentries followed her.

"May the light of the moon glisten on you, daughter of Mabon," Queen Kalani said, then ordered Willa to get her armor ready.

Romeo nuzzled against Tori's thigh. She reached for his head to pet him and met his puppy eyes. "I'm scared, Romeo. If I lose my family..."

"*You won't.*" Sada's voice echoed in Tori's head. "*Trust me. I might be acting hastily, but my father needs me to break him out of that spell before it's too late.*"

With that, Tori shut her eyes and took a deep breath before running out to join Sada in the courtyard.

Sada sat with her legs crossed in midair, her eyes closed. She kept her wrists on her lap and her chin high. From this angle, Tori could still see the young Avan's eyes straining to remain closed. Soon, Sada hummed musically, and a plum aura surrounded her body, glowing like the sun's corona during an eclipse. Her belly button shone like a star.

Queen Kalani stepped out of the broken castle walls,

dressed in her silver-white armor. Willa held the queen's shield with the Avan symbol. Galeno flew by, wings fluttering in unison with his army. His well-sculpted torso had a bruise from his previous fight. His armor and black hair glistened under the light.

Sada's body turned transparent, and Tori could see the trees behind her swaying with the breeze. Tori put her fingers over her mouth. A silence filled the courtyard, as if a movie had been paused.

The next second, Sada disappeared, and Mabon crashed onto the ground from a temporary portal like a wounded crow. His skin flushed raw, and half his armor was gone. He was breathing unevenly. Tori ran to him and placed the back of her hand on his forehead and cheek. He ran a high fever and showed no hint of recognition of anyone. He pushed her hand away multiple times.

Without any explanation, the queen raised her son off the ground; the blue dust sprawling from her fingers made a mattress under him, and she led the body indoors while Galeno dealt with the remaining guards on the grounds.

Galeno moved close to Tori and said, "Casualty of war, my dear."

CHAPTER
23

Camille wiped the dirt off her nose and watched a bright light form in the middle of the cave. As it grew brighter, she couldn't watch it anymore. Aja moved away from the light and stepped onto crumbled rocks. Her bare feet scraped, bleeding a strange color hard to pinpoint under the brilliance. Aja's cry was followed by an echo, the Garghon witch tried to calm down but only succeeded in making her grumble incoherently.

Soon, Camille realized what happened: Mabon's body was gone, and in his place was Sada, sprawled on the floor. The young Avan opened her eyes and rolled to her side. She reached for something on her back and panicked.

"Sada!" Camille went to the princess while the beast tended to her wounds. "What have you done?"

Sada looked up at her mentor, then around the rock walls in the cavern. Her body trembled from the cold. "It worked," she chuckled.

"Of course, it worked." Camille helped her up.

"It was the only way to get my father to safety," Sada said quietly.

Camille nodded and noticed the beast turn in their direction, Tamesis following suit.

"We'll discuss this later," Camille said matter-of-factly, and she waved her arms like branches in a breeze. She formed an orange glow before dispersing rays toward their opponents.

With a swift caress, Sada tilted her head back and summoned enough energy into her hands. She molded the blue energy into a darker brown on her palm and flashed a sandstorm in the shape of a hawk toward the beast, causing it to whimper and fall on its knees.

"I think you just made her angrier, dear princess." Camille manifested a shield and secured it to her forearm.

"Good."

The two Avans got ready to fly, but Sada made fists and pressed her eyes closed to no avail. "I can't fly!"

"This is your chance! Destroy them," Tamesis growled.

Aja spread her arms wide and raised herself. "You took him away," she hissed, and she threw knife-like rays toward the Avans. Some ricocheted to the ceiling. Rocks tumbled down, hitting their shoulders and heads.

Sheltering the princess, Camille kept the materialized shield over them, and Sada knelt. The rubble smelled fiercely like clay and moss.

Sada curled her finger, making a blue ball. Camille nodded, and Sada stood, throwing the ball at the beast. It hit its pelvis, making its naked skin squirm like ripples on water.

"You dare!"

Tamesis cursed under her breath. Sparks built on her talons. She spit them onto the Avans, hitting their calves, making them trip and wince.

"The two of you are good," Tamesis said with a twinkle in her yellow eyes. "But *we* are better."

"The amulet, Sada." Camille limped back, produced another shield, and handed it to Sada. "I've been trying to get it, and each time I met resistance."

Sweat fell on Sada's forehead. Purple veins formed on the area where the darts stung. They crawled up her thigh.

"You deal with the Garghon." Sada passed her hand over her leg; a thin film traced it, and the veins disappeared along with the dart. She turned to Camille and did the same. "The beast has weakened. I need someone to cover my back in case we need to escape."

Camille nodded. She understood the reason Sada needed to deal with Aja. That last finger magic spell was Oda's. He had to be guiding her. She pulled her sleeves up to her elbows, preparing for the onslaught they were about to unleash. She and Sada looked at one another, ready to send their magic at Tamesis and Aja. Their shields lit up like pinwheels, spinning nonstop. Their staffs had an arrowhead at the tip, which glowed like fire burning on a bush.

"Whatever happens, know that I am proud of you." Camille raised her staff, and the fire traveled above her head.

"You say that as if this were your last battle." Sada creased her brow.

Camille turned away. "If there is a life worth saving, it is Ava's link to the past now that Oda is gone, Princess."

And before Sada could reply, she watched Camille face the enemy. The same determination she had seen in training. Urmi was right to say her mother had a plan. She was here, fulfilling her duty as promised.

Once Camille swung her staff, Tamesis conjured a spell to throw at them, and Aja displaced her anger by creating tiny critters crawling on the side of the wall. Their beady eyes were fixed on their prey.

"That's not good." Camille's heart skipped a beat, and she took a breath to calm herself.

Sada lifted her shield and made it invisible. "I'll deal with Aja." She jumped on a boulder and swung her staff at the critters.

Aja screeched and levitated toward the Avan, wrapping her growing hair around the girl's neck, pulling her down, and dragging her sideways.

"Finish her," Tamesis ordered.

Aja's fingers turned bony white, and her hair grew thicker.

"Oh, you would want that," Camille said, running toward the Garghon witch. She knocked the witch down and pounded her with the shield.

Tamesis took hold of the weapon, and her talons sank deep into it, causing it to crumble.

The ashes touched Camille's forearm and seared her skin. She stepped back and clutched her arm. An overwhelming heat pressed on her skin, stinging and tainting. The smell of burned flesh circled her.

"Now you are ugly, and no Avan will want a scarred witch." Tamesis laughed as she stood and kicked the ashes toward Camille.

Camille stepped back to avoid the vexed ashes and narrowed her eyes. She covered her tender arm. Softly, she uttered the spell for a makeshift armor strengthened of fine linen and aloe vera to protect her wound.

"Mates don't have to kiss the scars," she whispered, and she crossed her fingers and made a circle counterclockwise over the ashes that remained from her shield. A dust cloud filled with the crystals from the dirt surfaced and formed a stone bird. The bird was shaped like an eagle, and as the top surface broke off, it flew straight at Tamesis.

The Garghon witch covered her face as the eagle pecked at her exposed, charred skin, breaking some of her armor and pulling her coarse hair. She tried grabbing the bird, but only managed to get cut.

Meanwhile, Aja tugged at Sada, who struggled to break free of her grip. The critters covered the Avan and formed a cocoon after Aja pushed down on Sada's trachea.

The darkness was a close friend of Sada's, and she closed her eyes, slowing her heart and breathing. She heard the ocean miles away through the thick rock of the volcano. She heard the clashing metal of Avan and Garghon like distant voices. She watched the eagle peck at Tamesis. She saw her brothers... Gasping, she opened her eyes. She needed to escape to help

Camille. Aja was going to strike her down. She couldn't let her mentor die. She summoned Oda's magic and enveloped herself with it. Her body glowed like the stars in space, pushing the critters off her body and smashing them against the wall.

Aja sent a death bolt hurling toward Sada. Sada blocked the bolt with her open palm, absorbing it.

Camille blinked repeatedly. Nothing had come out behind Sada's hand, which meant the girl had a protective shell around her.

The beast widened her eyes in disbelief, then dug her heels into the ground and conjured up another death bolt for the young Avan who took her prized king.

Realizing the beast was going to strike, Camille sent her own magic bolt to Aja, hitting the beast's back and knocking her over. Sada used her powers to break off pieces of rock from the walls and started to encase Aja within them.

Tamesis finally managed to get the eagle off her by chaining it inside a makeshift cage with a spell. She hissed and watched the beast crawl on her hands and knees. The Avans were reaching for the amulet. She ran toward them, but an invisible wall stopped her. She pounded the wall with her fists and clawed at it. Only sparks flew onto her tattered clothes and wounded arms. Turning toward an exit where the rocks were pulled off, she had no choice but to relay the details of the battle to King Waqar and hope the boy prince was ready, even if she only had half the spell for the transformation. At least there was still time to take her pretty mess and flee.

CHAPTER
24

Quoba and the Avan army weren't prepared to find Prince Mabon gone or the casualties from both parties on the beach. Holding his breath while he landed, Quoba stared at the bodies of his fellow soldiers. The sound of battle from a few miles away brought Quoba back to focus. The Garghons had the Avans pinned near a stretch of land under an overhanging cliff to easily stop them from flying out. Galeno would have led this army to victory and expected his warriors to follow in his footsteps. The blood spilled on the beach reminded Quoba of the ancient sayings of a battle in which the Avans would lose their world. But that was for the end of time, not the beginning of it. Oda had said the twin princes were part of that beginning.

"What would you like us to do?" An Avan soldier flew near Quoba. His helmet was dented and stained from their previous battle. The stain inhibited the gleam from their splendid armor under the rising sun.

Quoba lowered his eyes from the stupor of finding the island with the bodies of his comrades and said, "We take them."

The soldier placed his fist over his chest and nodded.

Raising his eyes, Quoba added, "Flank the Garghons and crush the remaining enemy before they do us."

The soldier turned and relayed the orders to the rest of

the army with the flags. In turn, they drew their weapons and adjusted their helmets.

The two Avans who had carried Gabriel to the island set him down behind a line of Avan soldiers before flying back up to meet the ones who would deal with the aerial assault.

Gabriel wiped his chin and bit the side of his lip. The sun had come out, and he found himself straining to see past the Garghons' askew faces as they bared their teeth and raised their weapons. The Avans' wings were gone for a moment until needed. That was how they could easily blend into his world. The ones above already had their wings, each with their own colorful feathers that made them distinct. They headed toward the Garghons with the first strike. Though the Garghons liked to break the rules, they knew better than to do battle in the air with their heavy armor and weapons, especially since the Avans were superior flyers.

A wind swept the metallic scent of blood to Gabriel's nostrils, and he looked down at the sand again. Trails of blood from both parties stained the beach. He clutched his throat while his stomach churned. After the years he lived on Ava, he knew he would never be like them. Some reminded him of that fact, and now he saw his fallen comrades. He recognized most soldiers training for the moment their queen needed them. Yet he couldn't help but relive the scenes of his parents' deaths. His father's frightened face as he plunged down into the battle pit where Sada fought Nafuna. And his mother...

Quoba blew the battle horn, causing Gabriel to shiver at the loud, brash sound, and the Avans marched forward while the aerial group hovered above, providing a brief shade. Gabriel stepped on the dry blood as his knee buckled from stepping on an indentation in the sand. He clutched at the sand, and he forced the tears to stop consuming him. *Would this be the place where he took his last breath?*

"Are you okay?" A gray-eyed Avan soldier placed his hand on Gabriel's shoulder. He recalled the name to be Declan—

someone Sada had consulted with in regards to some herbs for minimizing pain.

With a determined look, Gabriel nodded. He rose and grabbed hold of the shield hooked to his back. It weighed heavily on his arm. "Which way?" He took a fighting stance.

"Quoba wants this line to the left," the Avan said with a frown forming under his long black hair, which had a hint of chestnut. It was in a ponytail that the wind swept when he turned in the direction ordered. "We're to hold off until reinforcements arrive," Declan said after reading the signals given by the flags.

But before Gabriel could answer, half of the Garghons over-ran the line in front of them and made their way towards the rear. Gabriel held his breath and exhaled. He drew his sword along with the Avan, waiting for them to get close enough. The volcano behind them and the orange-tinted sky painted a serene scene, contrasted by the red plum blood smeared on the sand. The lack of flowers and birds also made him gulp at his turn to battle. All he could do was survive, if that were possible for a human in the midst of such superior creatures.

As the wind kicked up the sand on the Avans' faces, Gabriel was almost caught off guard by the Garghon lifting his club, but he fouled off its attack by slicing through the creature's knees. The screeching sound overpowered the other battle cries, and Gabriel swerved to the creature's right and jabbed its back with the pommel of his sword, making it crash on the sand.

Another Garghon rushed forward. He knocked Gabriel down and managed to kick him in the ribs. A cursing pain soared through Gabriel's body, and he tried to protect himself with the shield to no avail. The pain intensified, and he felt his armor giving way as the third kick hit his rib. He was power-less to stop it, and the gray-eyed Avan had his own Garghons to deal with to be able to lend a hand.

"Gabriel!" Quoba's voice bellowed from a short distance.

Gabriel's body shot up like a stuffed toy a dog grabbed as he was tossed aside when the Garghon rammed his leg into him again. He no longer felt the pain, only the vision of his childhood with his family scrawled in the sky. *They were riding horses down the slopes behind the farm. The leaves on the trees fell on them as they passed. The air was pure, and the sun nurtured his skin.*

"Gabriel!"

The voice again...

"Wake up!"

Gabriel opened his eyes and found Quoba holding his head. He tasted the iron from the blood filling his mouth and sensed the ache piercing his side like a knife. He heard the Avans disarming the Garghons and keeping them at bay. Sweat droplets fell off Quoba's forehead, landing on his cheek.

"Did... we win?"

Quoba set Gabriel's head down on the cold sand and inspected the young man's side by gently removing the warped armor chest plate.

Gabriel winced and watched the clouds rush past them. For a moment, he thought of Sada, *holding her close and tasting her sweet lips... her body pressed against him in a tender embrace, hot... both of them wanting each other but never fulfilling the urge...*

"Wake up, Gabriel!" Quoba slapped him.

Groggy and throbbing, Gabriel moaned.

"The fight's not over, my friend." Quoba tore part of the flag they carried and placed it on Gabriel's side, tying it around. "But you're staying out of it for now."

Shaking his head, Gabriel said, "No... I have to..."

"You don't have to prove yourself to me."

Sighing, Gabriel winced. "No... for her..."

An Avan ran to them and saluted with his left fist on his chest. "Sir, the Garghons are sending reinforcements."

"No more argument," Quoba ordered, returning the flag to

the bearer. "You'll be picked up soon."

"Sir!" Another Avan fell from the sky. His wings burned and his limbs twisted on the sand.

Quoba swallowed and placed his hand over Gabriel's chest. "You have your demons, and I have mine, my friend. For now, I must deal with them."

CHAPTER
25

Xio knew that if he gave in to the dark magic, there would be no turning back, but the pull weakened him, and it got harder to find his way, even with Xander's help. He recalled how he and his brother both underwent the same scrutinizing lessons about magic. The importance of keeping it under control and the mark it left behind. Though they had a lot to learn as their powers increased, they weren't the same boys from the farm. Play time was replaced by combat training. They didn't ask for the secrets to burden their new life. After that last shift in his appearance, Xio's body had a mind of its own, and he didn't like it. His skin was blackened, and his back ached from the stumps rubbing on his shirt as if something heavy had been pointed at it repeatedly.

The sound of nails dragging rattled Xio, and he looked up from where he lay on his side. He noticed his brother in chains, arms pulled behind him, and a thick metal choker around his neck. His eyes watered at the sight, and he forced his pain aside to focus on Xander for a moment. His eyes were less bright, and his hair never looked this messy. *Neither of us asked to be here, brother.* Xander's thoughts echoed in his, but Xio wanted to end it. End his torment in any way possible—to return to the farm, learn to breathe again, and forget his destiny.

Xander blinked, and Xio turned away. *Could Xander read*

my cowardly thoughts? With that, the itchy stumps pushed out, tearing the clothing further. Small wings unfolded until they fully emerged, splitting his shirt open, and his body convulsed. He bit the neckline, his teeth grinding down on the sweat, and the pain in his back intensified.

"Finally." King Waqar flew down from atop the rocks, where he overlooked the fighting outside in the safety of the volcano. Sending fire bolts to aid his army when he found the need. He took hold of Xander's chains and tugged on them like a steer.

Xander couldn't speak, for the metal wrapped around his neck was big enough to keep his jaw taut, but he could see. He could see the charred bat-like wings of a Garghon on his brother. He could see the dry charcoal skin on his brother's back, the eyes like a raven. At least his brother still resembled a boy. A boy whose fear could be his undoing.

"What did you do?" Xander projected onto the king.

"Surprised, chick?" King Waqar replied to Xander's directed thoughts. Then he summoned his servant and dropped the chains. "Find Tamesis and the scum she covets. We must complete the spell in his prime."

The Garghon bowed and scurried out of the cavernous room they were in.

Xander looked at the king's cold throne and the huge ceiling leading to a different vent. Someone would find it eventually. These heavy chains were encased with a locking spell. There had to be a way to break free of them. He needed time to think. His brother depended on him. *For how long?* He wasn't sure, but he had to keep them from fully completing Xio's conversion.

A dark shadow moved within the vent, and Xander blinked repeatedly to try and see who it was. The scarred arms of a Garghon revealed the visitor.

"Tamesis," King Waqar said with a hint of pride. "The book?"

Tamesis knelt and bowed her head; her yellow eyes moved from side to side, clothes torn, and scratches on her flesh.

The king sniffed the air, raised his hand, and struck the witch's torso. Her body zoomed past Xander and hit the side of a rock table. As she gathered her wind, the king pulled her up by her unruly hair and brought her to his angry face.

"You'd better have a good reason for failing, Tamesis."

Gulping, the witch replied, "Your highness, the young Avan warrior training under Oda has arrived."

King Waqar let Tamesis fall. He curled his lip at the news. "Proceed."

"The Avan prince was under Aja's spell when Sada came in and made him disappear."

"And the book?"

Licking her lips, she said, "The two sorceresses have the beast tethered." She backed away from the king; his shadow loomed over her. "But I *can* complete the spell."

He scratched under his chin and looked back at the twins. Steam blew out of his nostrils in a fury, like a bull ready to run. "And yet the boy has wings. Make him whole."

"Yes. Yes, mighty one."

Then, the Garghon King leaned over her and added, "If he isn't mine before nightfall, I will crush your bones and feed them to the Garghon army."

Tamesis let out a nervous smirk. "The boy will be yours, Great One."

"Good. And since you have such confidence in the spell without the book, try it on your pet." King Waqar extended his arm, and part of the rock wall split open. "Nothing must go wrong with the boy."

Snarling, Tamesis made fists, and the yellow of her eyes turned red.

The Garghon servant pushed Edouard through the opening. The Avan stumbled inside. His leg was severely bruised, one of his wings was partly plucked, and the side of his face was swollen.

"You have no right to treat an Avan with disrespect!" Xander echoed in the Garghons' heads. Each cowered forward from the vibration.

Rage built in King Waqar's face, and he pulled on the chains holding the boy, tugging until he dragged Xander halfway to the center of the Doom Room.

Without the ability to open his mouth, Xander could not scream the agony caused by the rocks scraping against his body; only a muffled echo accompanied his brother's loud cry, which equaled the roaring of an avalanche.

Edouard raised his good eye and spotted Xio's new wings and skin color. "What have you done?"

"Don't worry, pretty mess." Tamesis climbed the rocky steps toward the Avan. She grabbed his hair and pulled his head back.

Edouard grunted.

"We're going to need you to try something."

CHAPTER
26

Mabon wiped his forehead with a cool compress, letting it soothe his burning skin. He found the queen's hand and brought it to his lips. The citrus and floral scent of the flower, *Bird of Paradise*, touched his nose. He kissed her hand and let go.

"Thank you, mother."

"My son," she lengthened the sounds of each word, "you're quite welcome."

He opened his eyes and met the queen's blue ones, which shone along with her smile. "Have I been gone long?"

She brushed his hair back with her fingers. "Long enough to smother my heart."

Mabon caressed his mother's cheek with the back of his hand. It wasn't often they were alone, and he wanted to let her know how much he loved her.

"There isn't much time." She caught his fingers and set them down. "Sada has gone to help Camille with the beast."

"Wh—"

She rested her hand on his chest to stop him from rising. "*They* will deal with the beast. *You* have an army battling the Garghons. The few who remain on Ava will protect it."

"Galeno has built a strong fort?"

"Of course." She removed the compress and set it on the table. Her graceful neck, like a swan's, reminded Mabon of a ballet dancer; her movements were choreographed to the way she folded the cloth.

"What else?" he sighed.

"You must be well to stop the Garghon's plans."

He propped himself up with his elbows. "What else?"

The smile soon disappeared, and the sparkle of the eyes darkened as if preparing for an ominous speech. Finally, she said, "King Waqar has the princes."

Mabon leaped out of the bed, then sank back on its edge as an overwhelming dizziness took hold of his body.

"Take it slow, my son. You have yet to recharge all of your strength."

"I must go after them," Mabon said, massaging his forehead. That's when he detected that his skin had marks as if he had run through a field of barbed wire.

"What happened to me?"

Tori walked through the makeshift door to the safe room, bringing more water. The sight of her husband struggling to balance against the bed caused her to drop the bowl. She ran to him, hugging him and taking in the musky scent of the man she loved. The scent of work, spice, and fresh spring.

"I've missed you." She let go and met his dual-colored eyes. She looked into each one and saw the brutal fear she had when she found out about their sons. She set her palms on his bruised cheeks. "Are you okay?"

But Mabon couldn't respond. His body grew cold, and his head spun with the images of his battle with King Waqar years ago, how Ibis forced his children to develop their powers too early, and how the Avans were reluctant to have him on Ava. He relinquished Tori and turned back to his mother. "Where's Galeno? We need a plan to free the twins."

Queen Kalani nodded. That's when Mabon realized the queen wasn't well. Her wings had less sparkle, and her face was ashen. He looked at Tori, whose face was lined with worry and concern, and he said in a soft voice, "Can I speak with the queen alone, please?"

Tori placed her hand on his chest. She wanted to alleviate the evil done by the beast and the anger building inside him. It was a hurt she wasn't accustomed to dealing with. Ever since she met him, he had been respectful, composed, and sweet.

"Tori?"

"I love you, Mabon," she said, taking his hand. "I want to be part of bringing back our sons."

He leaned down to kiss her cheek and whispered in her ear, "You are the air I breathe."

The words filled her with hope, and she eased back to gaze at his face. A face that had hardly aged. There was warmth and determination written on it, but she knew war came before wife, and what mother and son would share dates back centuries before her time. She nodded reluctantly. "I'll be with Urmi and Willa." She turned to bow to the queen before departing.

Queen Kalani stood and walked toward the broken window, shattered by the Garghon intrusion a while ago. "Time is running, son."

"You once asked me to be king, mother."

Her hair bounced on her shoulders as she turned to Mabon. "Yes."

"Why don't you grant me the opportunity to understand?" He extended his hands.

Lowering her eyes, she gazed back at the garden where it was trampled by soldiers. "I'm not sure what you're referring to."

"When we returned to Ava from your exile, you had to slay Waqar's mate. Do you know what that cost us?"

The queen regarded her son and watched as his noiseless movements toward her reminded her of Gerardo; the way he would tease her when he wanted to ask a favor that she wouldn't be too fond of. Gerardo was nonjudgmental about her wings. When his rough hands draped around her, they made her feel complete. It was strange that such a thought would enter her mind. She usually kept those feelings about her mate hidden.

"Waqar's anger has lasted since before your time," she finally replied.

"Why? Why are the Garghons so hell-bent on killing us?"

Silence.

Mabon placed his palm over his aching stomach. Whatever the beast had done to him, it made his skin pulse. "I know my father learned the Avan ways long before he died, and I know you think of him now."

She raised her eyes.

"We are linked through him." He touched his chest, pointing to his heart and where the Eye of Zorea merged. "He's with me. Inside. I bear the burn mark from the union with the medallion Oda gave me."

A tear rolled down Queen Kalani's cheek. "Then, you know."

"I know your powers have dampened again, but at your will."

A slight wind rustled the leaves outside like little feet scurrying and tumbling over the garden.

Walking up to his mother, Mabon asked, "What I don't know is why the Garghons return time and time again to wreak havoc upon us."

She took hold of Mabon's hand. "The Garghons are born from death, son. They are the remains of what Avan and humans once were. They are the souls of the darkness within each corpse. They cannot reproduce, and the more casualties you give them, the more Garghons there will be. It is a sickness that must be stopped."

Mabon took his mother's other hand and held it firmly. "The Garghons feed on death. I know, mother. What can my children offer differently?"

"It's not what they can present; it's what they can do."

Mabon squeezed her hands and felt an electric shock pulse through his fingers. A few seconds later, he was enveloped in a haze. He saw bodies lying atop bodies... Avan, human, Garghon... and above the carnage were two beings hovering.

One with black wings and the other with wings as radiant as his mother's. Mabon let go of the queen's hands and shook his head to clear the images she shared.

"Are you saying my sons will bring destruction?

"Not the end." She waved her hand in dismissal.

"I don't understand." He creased his brow.

"They are the balance the universe needs to bring a new beginning. Without each other, they will be placed at each other's throats, and none will stop them."

"I think we're getting ahead of ourselves. They are only children."

"Children with an uncanny ability to harness power."

Mabon stepped back and glanced at his mother's paleness. The luster in her hair was almost gone. He couldn't fathom being without her again after finally being able to come home. Still, she wasn't telling him everything. Then a thought occurred to him. "You gave your powers to one of them. You gave them to Xander."

"I will not be here for the final test of his ability to manipulate them. You must teach him." Her voice cracked, and she cleared her throat.

"Why did you do it?"

Before she could answer him, her fragile body collapsed back in mid-air, changing into a rainbow assortment of stars that dispersed with the next wind.

CHAPTER
27

Without the amulet, the beast was overpowered by Sada and Camille. They tied Aja to a chain made of magical steel to prevent her from escaping. Aja shifted back to her monstrous state, drooling and biting the chain keeping her prisoner.

Stains of dirt and sweat smeared on both Sada and Camille's cheeks, shoulders, and arms. They took a brief moment to collect themselves from the smell building on their bodies, enhancing the moldy walls. Glancing around the dreary cavernous room, they were exhausted from the feat and hot from the exertion. Each of them thought of their families, hoping all was well.

Opening the amulet in half, a lavender light emerged, shining on Camille's face. Once she broke it down further, it turned into a hefty book. The book's edges were creased and worn. A single silver feather was etched in the center of the used black cover.

"There's no time to lose," Camille said. "I'll return this to Ava and make sure it hasn't fallen."

"Trust me, it hasn't." Sada wiped her forehead and concentrated on forming her wings. She closed her eyes and made fists as if straining to see beyond the stars for the first time. She could feel her triceps harden and her shoulder blades pull back, but nothing happened.

Camille placed her hand on Sada's back. "Without them, you are still whole, princess."

"An Avan without their wings that could no longer fly or use their magic to materialize new ones?" Sada said woefully.

Camille saw the concern in Sada's eyes, and she softened her features. "I know…"

"I don't understand why." Sada sighed.

"The answer will have to wait." Camille rose and dusted the book's cover, exposing the glitter-like surface. "You have the advantage of being able to stealthily find your way to your brothers."

The echo of a horrid scream traveled into their cavern, consuming the walls and stopping their breathing as it moved further down like an invisible wave. Each spun around and found the beast still chained, but the screams wouldn't stop.

Closing her eyes, Sada concentrated on the sound, and her fleeting heart pumped. "The twins!"

"Go!" Camille took hold of Sada's hand and squeezed it. "I will inform the Avans outside."

"Secure the book on Ava." Sada squeezed her fists again.

Camille nodded. "Trust in your abilities, dear one, for without the confidence to face the nightmare ahead, you will lose more than flight."

Without turning back, Sada ran past the beast and through the tunnel, using Oda's power bestowed on her to sense the direction in locating her brothers' distinct power signatures. All the while repeating Camille's cryptic words.

"You birds will find the end of my club deadlier than your sword." Baqir scraped the spikes on his club against Jaime's arm.

Jaime let out a screech and fell back, hugging his arm to his chest. His skin, yellowish at the fingertips, contrasted his bronzed tone.

Quoba watched in disgust as what used to be a man kicked his legs from the pain, long teeth protruding from his lips, then turned back to Baqir. "You think you have us at a disadvantage, but we have seen your magic outshined before."

The Garghon leader bellowed crass remarks and lifted his club to give the attack command, but Quoba rammed at him with all his strength against the four other Garghons behind him. The rest of the Avans followed suit and proceeded to unsheathe their swords. Not holding back, the Garghons echoed their leader's call and ran forward, colliding with the sand and their enemies.

A swarm of Avans flew down and grabbed the shoulders of some Garghons. They struggled to break free of their grasp, but the Avans held firmly onto the creatures' shoulders with a clasp, taking them high and letting them fall into the volcano or water.

The Garghons that weren't carted off cried in anger and doubled their weapons. A sword and flail were used to battle their adversaries.

Quoba pushed down with the blade of his sword, but Baqir managed to push the hefty Avan off him. Securing his club, Baqir readied to strike, but Jaime took the club away from behind, biting into the handle.

"Maybe your Garghons would like to convert as he has." Quoba pressed his elbow on Baqir's throat.

The Garghon leader pushed Quoba off again and stood. "You will pay for that, Avan pig!"

Another soldier provided his leader with a sword, and Baqir posed, ready for the next bout. Licking his lips at the prospect of victory, Baqir shifted his stance and slid his club under two Avans, then swerved it toward Quoba, striking the giant Avan in the stomach.

Quoba bounded back and coughed. Raising his sword, he ran at the Garghon and maneuvered his weapon sideways to slide the blade against the creature's neck, but Baqir bent his body backwards, kicking up his legs and breaking Quoba's chance to slice. Four other Garghons flew down on top of Quoba, stepping on his arms and grabbing onto his wings' bases to pull. He let out a winded, gruff sound as his face and chest hit the salty sand. The other Avans knew the reason Quoba had two different colored wings and realized what the creatures planned to do with their superior. Letting out a battle cry, the Avans created a club to go along with their sword and struck down as many Garghon warriors as they could.

Surprised at the rage the Avans emitted, the Garghons strived to stay in line.

Four Garghons subdued Quoba and pulled his arms back, keeping him taut for Baqir, who sauntered toward him. He lifted Quoba's chin, holding it firm in his talons.

"What do you say now?"

Narrowing his eyes, Quoba strained to break free. He heard his brothers and sisters fighting to the death. The clash of shields and metal clanged on like a recently broken stone. He ingested the scent of wet wood from the sea, pieces scattered by the shore, and he remembered Gabriel's face as he left him in the care of the healer. Hope outshone his wounds, and Quoba wanted nothing more than to bring Gabriel that hope for another day.

Baqir squeezed the Avan soldier's chin further. "I'm sure your warriors will cease this fight if I slice through your flesh. What about it?" He turned the Avan's head from side to side.

"What's the matter? Garghon, got your tongue?" and he filled the air with his laughter.

"No more!" the voice in the back of Baqir said, but before the Garghon could turn, a sharp object punctured a hole through his side, making him lose his grip on Quoba.

As blood dripped from his mouth, Baqir took hold of the spear, turned and met Jaime's crimson eyes, and pulled it out, swinging it around with one arm and pushing it through Jaime's heart.

CHAPTER
28

Mabon reached for his mother's remains as they floated away with the wind, joining Oda and the countless Avans who had lost their lives. If he didn't stop the war from escalating, countless others would lose theirs. He pressed his palm over his eyes and took hold of the bed frame in the room he was in. He knew he couldn't pull back his mother's aura. She had given it willingly to Xander, which meant Xander already knew of her passing or would sense it soon enough.

Massaging his forehead, he closed his eyes and committed his mother's scent to memory before it faded along with her. He could faintly hear her asking him to be strong. To be king. He exhaled, and his chest tightened. After another breath, he snapped his fingers, and the armor he lost at the Garghon stronghold reappeared, glistening at its softly curved edges. His throat continued to press against itself as he strapped it on. His mother was the first Avan to put the armor on him. The first to train him to fly. The first to cry on his father's passing. As he fastened it together, Romeo entered the room. His tail was tucked between his legs. A massive Belgian Shepherd who had been with him for years on the farm before he got married to Tori and was the closest thing to a best friend.

Mabon knelt on one knee and passed his injured hands over the dog's smooth coat until the tail relaxed. "So, you know, my old friend."

Romeo licked Mabon's hand, his glossy eyes meeting the king's, expressing all the trust and love a being could give.

"Her time had ended." Mabon returned his gaze to the few remnants of his mother floating away. "Now, it is my time."

A faint glow by the bed emerged, and Romeo whined before letting his mouth fall open and his tongue roll out, which meant it wasn't dangerous. In a way, Mabon knew what it was, but he couldn't bring himself to even think about it.

Mabon massaged the dog's left ear and watched as the glow moved past them like a detached candle down the hall. There was a warmth similar to the sun at first light. They followed it to the queen's chambers, where it went through the double doors. Halting, Mabon asked the guards to summon their commander, Galeno. He placed his hand over the peacock's feathers on the door, tracing the plumage. He let a tear fall.

Romeo nudged Mabon and tapped his nose against the door.

Waving his hand over the birds, he opened the doors and they went through. The faint glow remained on the wall beside his mother's large mirror. Mabon didn't want to be there. He didn't want to remember and let the feelings cloud his judgment during war, but he saw her hairbrush neatly placed on the table and the spell book she had shown Sada.

The glow brightened, and Mabon set his helmet down and parted the walls to his mother's secret compartment. Inside, the shimmering crown was placed on a soft mantel behind a glass cabinet.

With a faint yip, Romeo got on his hind legs and used his teeth to pry open the small latch. The glow disappeared, and Mabon took hold of the crown.

"My king." Romeo bowed.

Putting the crown back, Mabon closed both the cabinet door and the parted wall. "Not yet, my friend."

Romeo let out a quiet woof.

"Sometimes I wonder if you can read minds, too," Mabon said.

Romeo's lips curled on the left side.

"What is the meaning of this?" Galeno stood in full armor by the doorway with his hand on his sword's pommel.

Romeo sat by Mabon's side, his lips lowering, and grumbled.

"Queen Kalani has safely hidden away from Garghon eyes," Mabon said. "Not even *I* can contact her."

Galeno stepped inside; his footsteps came down hard as he marched through the room. "The queen always lets his general know of her whereabouts."

"We can't take any chances with the Garghons having broken through our defenses. Twice."

Galeno veered toward the prince. "If you're at the point of blaming someone, blame yourself, Your Eminence." He shortened the distance between them, crossing a large trunk whose contents had made the lid remain partly open. "Things haven't been going well since that last tactical command."

Creasing his forehead, Mabon stood tall and replied, "I'm not going to prove my qualifications to you or anyone on Ava. I summoned you here to relay the queen's message and for you to state what has been done with the flock."

Raising an eyebrow, Galeno let go of his sword. "The flock is secure, except for able-bodied Avans willing to fight. The army surrounds entry points, the rest around the castle."

"Good."

Romeo's eyes never left Galeno's, and his ears were so erect that the hairs in them stood on end.

"The princes have been captured." Mabon stepped back and glanced at the chandeliers above them, the same ones his sons had climbed a year ago before Tori put a stop to it. They had recently been cleaned by Willa. Regaining his composure, he continued, "Camille, Sada, Quoba, and his army are on the island. Any news?"

"News?" Galeno scoffed. "Those creatures have no intention of returning the princes, your highness." Galeno waved his hand in the air and turned, slamming his fist on his open palm.

"They await our destruction. We must act now."

"I can't leave Ava unattended, Galeno."

"While I am left out of this unholy war, your flock is massacred below," Galeno retorted.

"The key is already on the island."

Both Mabon and Galeno turned to face Camille in the doorway, while Romeo trotted to her side. Smudges of dirt and blood on her cheeks and arms didn't muffle her beauty. Her clothing was torn and shabby, along with her hair, but her vibrant blue-green eyes lovingly stared as peaceful lakes emanated.

Galeno made his way toward his mate, bowed, and kissed her hand gently. "I take it the beast is no more?"

It would be unnatural for Galeno to convey any emotion in front of Mabon, and Camille admired his self-control, but deep down, she felt her mate's distress. It wasn't often she entered a room filled with the filth of war. She faintly smiled and nodded, then, directing her attention to Mabon, said, "Sada is well. She makes her way to the princes' sides."

Mabon returned the greeting and asked, "You mentioned that the key is already on the island?"

"It's been there, biding time."

"Then use it, for we surely will rot without it," Galeno beckoned the prince.

"Then, it is not the book," Mabon said.

"The book and its dark magic are in our possession. Safe." Camille removed her hand from Galeno's and smoothed it over his cheek. He closed his eyes briefly. She continued, "The Garghons have the rest of the royal family, but *they* are the deadliest weapon cast by their own ignorance."

"Then it is true?" Galeno turned back to Mabon. "Oda had

spoken about the key to the Garghons' demise hidden within three cavities."

"All they need is to turn it," Camille said.

Mabon looked back to the wall where he had left the crown in place. "Hold the fort, Galeno. I must return to the island."

CHAPTER
29

If Sada didn't focus on her brother's screams, she would be lost in the Garghon stronghold's labyrinth. Much has changed since she was a prisoner and met Gabriel for the first time. Lucky for the creatures, the volcano was dormant, filled with tunnels and vents intertwining or ending abruptly. The island it sat on was lush enough for their tastes. Years ago, it was filled with sand and desert. Maybe her mother, Ibis, lent a hand in that, having been accustomed to an Avan setting. Yet, it didn't do anything for the thick stench of sweat and salt. The cold rock made Sada edgy, and she focused mentally on her brother's cry, which came louder to her left. Blindly, she trailed the carved wall with her fingers; the cold stone and dirt crumbled as she made her way to where the twins were held.

At the sight of Xio's transformation into a dark creature, Sada gasped. He was not fully into a Garghon; his hair and eyes were charcoal like a starless night. If it weren't for the whites of his eyes, you wouldn't notice his face. His human form was obvious as it stretched taller by another inch, except for the wings, which bent and expanded, hinting at a dark gray, which the red-brown rock around the large cavern enhanced. It was close to the direction King Waqar was going. Glancing over, Xander was chained. She could barely sense a new aura surrounding the boy, something not there before and hard to pinpoint. Calling on Oda's power, she closed her eyes and concentrated her thoughts on Xander. The hairs on the back of her neck stood up, and where her wings should be, they pressed on her back. She managed to reach Xander's mind without the Garghons realizing her presence.

In his chained state, Xander let out a breath as he felt the air vibrate around him. His eyes darted in the direction the sensation originated, knowing full well it was Sada. He kept his gaze locked on her location, to the far left of the vent, where she kept hidden. He let out a breath and sent a message of his own to her.

"Save Edouard. Xio is about to show off his new power."

Sada swallowed the air hitting her lips and held her breath as the message struck her brain like a coconut falling on top of her head. As the king shifted his body, she caught sight of Edouard being held by two creatures. The one in back of him was Tamesis. The witch had her eyes closed, and her lips moving. No sound came out, but Sada recognized she was trying the spell on him. Before she could fathom a plan, Xio's body rose from his crouched position.

"Let them all go," his husky voice boomed.

King Waqar belched a thunderous laugh, and the loose rock above fell as gravel rain.

"Tamesis will finish with her pet; then she'll finish you."

"No."

The boy stood with his legs shoulder-width apart. His left fist gave off a faint green glow radiating from inside his body. The mist flowed through him and out from the tips of his wings.

Growling, the king spread his wings wide. They appeared bigger from behind, with sharp claws and webbing sticking out from them. "Forget the pest, Tamesis."

Responding, she opened her eyes and noticed the transformed prince in a confrontational stance. "He is ready, my lord."

"Do it. Do it now!"

Raising her arms, Tamesis sent an electric net over the boy's head, but it faded through him like a shimmer.

"Impossible!" She focused her hand toward the boy and slowly curled each finger to squash the child. They turned black as she conjured the spell.

Nothing happened.

Edouard looked up as the creatures held on to his arms. His neck cracked, and a spasm followed in his back. Pain found itself in every part of his body. Yet he didn't seem to mind as he realized Xio was through playing helpless. Observing Xander, he could see the faint grin forming on his lips. This wasn't going to end well for the Garghons. If only he knew it would be for the princes.

Sada waited for a moment to see what Xander meant about their brother showing off his power before making her presence known. Tamesis' magic was having no effect on Xio, and the king's face wrinkled in disgust. Steam blew out of his nostrils, and his muscles tensed. He wasn't happy about the outcome.

"I'll subdue him myself, witch!" King Waqar flew up and remained hovering above Xio. His horns emitted short orange-blue sparks like a Jacob's ladder.

Xio raised his now-whitened eyes and flew up to meet the king's challenge. His lips curled, and the green glow increased on his fist into a spiral, forming a sword. Sada identified the Sword of Old from an image of it during a history lesson long ago. It was a weapon without a name. A weapon powerful enough to cut or kill whatever it touched. How could Xio summon it?

The prince passed his free hand over the blade and cut his palm. Then, squeezing his palm, the blood droplets fell on Xander's forehead below, trickling down to his neck. The metal collar on Xander broke open, and the chain followed. It crumbled onto the floor, turning into small green snakes.

Tamesis had the servants release Edouard and destroy the animals slithering up the walls toward the king. This gave Sada the opportunity to enter the cavernous room. Together, they could stop the king's plans and avoid more deaths. Though she could be of more use outside battling the remaining Garghon army, she wasn't sure if the princes were capable of handling a powerful warlock like King Waqar along with Tamesis. She had to find something in Oda's mind vault to help both causes.

As Sada made her way toward Edouard, Tamesis directed her attention there, too. After all, it was her pretty mess; she won fairly, and there were so many things she wanted to do to him before night came.

"So, you think you can take what belongs to me?" Tamesis hissed and rolled her forearms over each other, preparing a spell to use against the princess.

"I don't think anything, witch. I know."

Tamesis formed a magic sphere to toss at Sada, but before she could throw it, Xander used his magic to raise the Garghon off its feet and turn her upside down.

Tamesis shrieked in anger and wriggled, trying to break herself free.

"Thanks, brother." Sada waved her hand. "I'll deal with those two and get Edouard out."

"Not so fast," Tamesis bellowed, and she spun around until she got loose. Flying in place, she leered with her yellowed eyes.

"Maybe there's unfinished business here, witch, but I have no time." Sada directed her gaze toward the Garghon King above. "He might need your help, if you're willing to give it."

Tamesis turned and saw how the young Avan prince had the king tangled in a green neon web. She never saw the king defeated by anything.

Deep down, she relished the fact that the mighty king would be no more, but the other part of her knew a dead king meant dead leaders. Every Garghon with enough courage and strength replaces everyone, and she wasn't ready to give up her life yet.

CHAPTER
30

Baqir kept the spear firmly in Jaime's chest, whose face turned from pale to blue. The thought that a mere insect could surprise him with an attack was beyond measure. The horns that once occupied the human's head disappeared, and the blood that gushed out stopped. In a deliberate pull of the spear, Baqir released Jaime onto the ground, letting his body flop on the sand. The Garghons lavished at the sight and continued to press the Avans back from their leader, to which Baqir grinned.

Quoba pulled on the Garghons who held him, but it was too late. Jaime was dead. Quoba let his head hang to catch his breath. He wasn't going to let Baqir win. The Avans had never backed out of a fight. Deep inside, he trusted his queen and the royal family to get them out of this mess, but at the moment, it was up to him and his army. Raising his auburn eyes, he saw Baqir heading toward him. The Garghon formed a wry smile, and its armor covered only its right shoulder and bottom.

"Well, well, Avan scum." Baqir spun the spear in front of him. Jaime's blood dripped from the point down its side. "That human runt didn't have a chance since Tamesis laid her hands on him. What makes you so sure you can?"

"I believe."

After hearing those words, Baqir struck the Avan leader with the same spear he killed Jaime with.

The blood on it painted Quoba's cheek, touching his lips. The taste of human blood was as distinct as an Avan's, yet very much alike in its metal flavor, which could explain Prince Mabon's mixed lineage. Turning back to Baqir, Quoba stood tall and spit the blood from his mouth. The Garghons behind him tried to keep the large Avan down by his arms, to no avail.

Stepping back, Baqir ordered the soldiers to release the brute. He wiped the bloodied spit from his face and grabbed two swords. He threw one at Quoba, who caught it effortlessly. They each formed their battle stance and readied themselves.

With no mate, Quoba's ties remained with the kingdom. His whole life had been forged for this moment—defending the honor of Ava and all its inhabitants. He knew nothing else. Though if fate were to allow Willa to be by his side, he wouldn't shudder.

Baqir made the first move and lunged at Quoba, striking the Avan's side and slicing his skin, then striking the shoulder with a follow-up strike, making the brute bleed. Quoba followed suit and repeated the gesture, making sure to slice deeper. To his surprise, Baqir growled at the wounds and retaliated by smashing his sword against the Avan's. A few Garghons gathered on the sides with weapons in hand. If he could get the brute to fall, they would jump him.

As they fought, Quoba could hear his army battling the Garghons. The ensuing clash of metal and flesh bombarded the shore with its ominous melody, along with his. It lasted for minutes, then the ruckus and cheers of battle blew in like the wind, followed by the screams from the creatures. Glancing overhead, he saw the most magnificent set of white wings blocking the sun. The plumage was silky and bright, longer than previously, and it fit Prince Mabon well.

Baqir lunged again, this time inserting his sword into Quoba's side. "This is victory, pest!"

Catching a whiff of the creature's foul breath, Quoba grabbed his side where the pain shot up his torso and the muscles around the wound flexed tight, but his spirit was intact, so, with the other hand, he turned his sword around, keeping his grip on the pommel tight. "Not really." And he jumped, striking down on the creature's left pectoral, followed by a kick to the back of its legs.

The Garghon leader fell back as Quoba pushed down on the sword, which was angled to penetrate the creature's heart. Baqir raised a ruckus, pushing the sword away from himself and jabbing Quoba with his knee or punching the side where he inserted the sword until he could no more. Its yellowed eyes darkened, and its mouth remained agape, leaving the grimy teeth visible.

Quoba held the sword down for a few seconds more before removing it from the creature's body.

One by one, the Garghons dropped their weapons at the sight of Baqir's body and the presence of the majestic wings above. Their long faces had shadows filling their cheeks, their shoulders slumped, and their gait slowed. Guided by the Avans, they gathered near the summit as Mabon hovered down.

Kneeling, Quoba placed one fist against his chest; the other remained by his side. "Your highness. The Garghons have been defeated on this shore."

"Rise, my friend," Mabon said. He watched the large Avan wince as he hid the pain he felt from his wounds. Past Quoba, the Avan army fared well, but the casualties were many. His heart filled with sadness as he knew his role was to keep the flock afloat in this aftermath. Families and friends would be devastated and proud—a mix of feelings none of them would be able to express. A streak of orange lit the sky behind Quoba, and the ocean waves continued to foam on the shore. Mabon placed his hands over the Avan's deep wound. A dim blue light appeared, pulsing and warming his fingers.

When the light extinguished, Quoba didn't feel the stabbing pain, and the blood stopped. He looked down and saw the cut still there, beginning to seal.

"I only numbed the pain. There is much to be done, and I need you to help."

Nodding, Quoba said, "It is with honor I serve, my lord."

Mabon met the soldier's eyes, filled with concern.

"Gabriel..." Quoba gulped. "He is severely wounded, and his brother..." he turned.

As motionless as the rocks beside the summit, Jaime's body lay. His blood had stained the beach, and the hole from his wound made his skin stick to the clothes he wore. Mabon patted Quoba's shoulder. "I didn't know him very well, but what little Gabriel told me of him was enough to recognize he had a heart that loved his family, despite their differences." Then, he went to the body. The effects of the spell had gone with his spirit, and Jaime appeared human again. *Not much for conversation, but he played hard*, were the words his father said about Gabriel's brother. An ache stirred inside his chest, and Mabon formed a fist. War was senseless, and the truce the Garghons broke five years ago only brought more suffering. Jaime didn't deserve a death like this, but sometimes war was inevitable. Right had to be done.

Gathering his senses, Mabon declared, "All the dead must be gathered and taken back to Ava. Contact Galeno."

A breeze pushed Mabon's hair back and chilled his skin. He wasn't afraid of an unpleasant premonition, for the chill was his father and mother joining hands. Mabon's lips slid sideways, forming a lopsided grin. "Keep the Garghons restrained until you hear from me again."

"And you, my lord?"

"I have one more Garghon to deal with. I just hope I'm not too late."

CHAPTER
31

Sada unsheathed her sword and kept the Garghon soldier at bay, allowing one of the snakes the twins formed to escape through a shaft. From the corner of her eye, she spotted Edouard take the club away from the other Garghon servant. With his injuries, it was a miracle he even stood, but the teacher had always been known to persevere in all he did, a trait that came in handy in times like these.

Pulling the creature's horn back, she observed Xio hold King Waqar in his net, which made the king stew in anger, his body contorting as a bull ready to charge. Xander stretched his newly formed wings. They were a brilliant white with a spectrum, painting the rock wall behind them with their magic, like the aurora found at the North Pole. She was in awe at the sight when her father took her, and she was in awe now at the beauty of her brother.

The twins were opposites. Identical. Different. One.

The Garghon noticed the Avan's eyes retract back, exposing the whites. Without hesitation, he pushed her off and drew his club.

But Sada didn't need her vision to fight. She was skilled, and her enhanced powers gave her a new sight beyond normal vision. Though it clouded whatever stood in front of her, as if she were staring into the sun with an object at its center like an eclipse. The minute the creature yanked his horns from her hands, she lifted her sword to stop the club that followed.

The Garghon growled and tried pressing down on the weapon, except the sword grew white hot, tinged with the color orange, so blinding. He stepped back and shook his head.

Sada's eyes returned to their original bicolor. She blew on the sword, and it, too, returned to its original silver lining with the Avan symbol powerfully in gold.

"Maybe you should reconsider your tactic," she imparted.

The Garghon raised his club and snarled, lips curled over bare teeth. But before it could charge, two cone-shaped rocks flew down and struck him through the chest. Coughing up blood and its life force, the creature fell to its side and died.

Creasing her brow, Sada stared at the Garghon, whose body dripped blood from the intrusion. She looked up at Xio, and his free hand formed another cone to throw at the Garghon Edouard struggled with.

"No!" Sada jumped high, but without her wings, she couldn't reach Xio. The throne room was at the center of the volcano; thus, the ceiling was high. She was grounded. She grunted as her foot landed back on the stone.

Luckily, Tamesis disintegrated the new cones Xio was forming. She moved in to cut the net that held her king.

Xio turned his attention to her.

As Sada fell from her second attempt at reaching the prince, Xander created a giant hand out of rock with his mind. The floor below Sada shook and rumbled, and the hand protruded out of it, catching her in its palm.

"That's two I owe you, brother," she said, wiping her forehead. "What about Xio?"

Xander nodded and flew closer to his twin with such ease that Sada marveled at the sway of the new wings.

"Make the monster release my king!" Tamesis screeched. She looked up to find the prince's lips moving, and she dropped the blade from her hand as it grew searing hot from the prince's spell.

"Tell King Waqar the war is over," Xander said calmly, a hint of their father in his changing voice. He circled his arms, and a window to the setting outside showed Tamesis the Garghon army diverted to a corner for holding. The sun beating down on the battlefield made it hard to see them. But their sullen faces told of a distressing aftermath.

King Waqar gripped the net that bound him, surprised that his army had fallen on their land.

"That's a lie, runt." Tamesis glided towards the boy, her eyes narrowing. "Our army is the fiercest in this world. Not even the mighty Avans can stop us." She raised her arms and formed a cloud above her head. The walls grew damp, and she chanted an incantation as the ceiling started to crumble.

Realizing he was outmatched, the Garghon servant fled, running toward the exit to find out whether what the Avan showed was true. King Waqar lifted his arm to spear him for his cowardice, but the net projected the ray back to him.

Edouard weighed the club in his hand, gripping it tight. He took a deep breath, tensing his muscles. Exhaling, he ran toward the witch to stop whatever she planned.

Sada covered her head with a shield she manifested from the rocks to protect herself from the impact. When safe, she watched Edouard swing the club and strike Tamesis on the back.

Squawking, the witch snarled, "That will cost you, pretty mess!" She brought large rocks down, but this time, Xio trapped all of them in another green net and squeezed them together, forming a small dome. He hammered it on top of the witch, sealing her in.

Xander flew to Edouard and pushed him out of the way before more rocks fell on him, too.

"Thank you, my prince," Edouard said as he stretched his back from the stress. "But what are we going to do about Prince Xio?"

Wrinkling his forehead and peering at his brother above,

Xander let Edouard down. "It's not safe inside. Take Princess Sada and go."

Heaving a sigh, Edouard looked at the worry lines forming on the young prince. No child should have worry lines, but he understood this fight was between them.

"Yes, my prince." Edouard stood and limped forward.

Sada floated to them, having used her magic to turn a slab of rock into a flying surfboard for her transportation. "Is Tamesis..."

"No. I hollowed the center from the impact."

"She's trapped, then?" Edouard frowned. "I'm somewhat relieved." He massaged his bruised right shoulder.

"Come," Sada said, taking his arm and helping him onto the slab. "I'll drop you off outside with the wounded." She turned to Xander and watched the determination build on his face. Even now, she wanted to protect him, even though he wasn't that baby brother anymore. "I will return for you."

He looked at her squarely. "You won't."

"Little prince—"

The crashing of bones vibrated in the rubble, cut Sada off.

"Go," Xander pleaded.

Sada held her breath and nodded. Then, without much delay, hovered through a tunnel to the outside of the volcano.

CHAPTER
32

King Waqar pushed on the net surrounding him, but the web was made out of a thorny substance that pricked his dry skin. All he managed to do was get tangled even further, and at the prospect of appearing foolish, he stopped struggling. Instead, he observed the boy prince stiffen with each use of his magic, which might be a vulnerable point and an opportunity to strike. Tamesis hadn't completed the spell on Xio, and he exerted energy unlike the other Avans.

Decades ago, Waqar would not have found it strange. The Avan flock had always maintained a high level of magic capable of holding the universe afloat, whereas the Garghons were made of their remains, and magic was bestowed upon a few, forming a caste system he reveled in. Yet, the boy's powers were unparalleled, unless what Ibis managed to do was bring forth the latent abilities already in place. If so, changing the boy completely into a Garghon might mean the end of everything. Apparently, the boy could still think on his own and had no clue as to his true nature. Then there was the sword he held, which was now cradled on his back. What grand power would it hold?

"Xio, you need to let him go."

Waqar turned to the other twin and grinned. There was one weakness he could use against the boy, but he had to tread carefully, for the ancient powers of this brat were not known to him. Magic like that deserved more observation, which he couldn't afford time with.

Flying closer to his brother, Xander covered his face as Xio brightened the cavern with an intense light that warmed Xander's skin like water vapor. He needed to make sure Xio understood by talking some sense into him before the power consumed him. And before he used the added magic the queen gave him against what his brother had become.

Within the net, the king shifted to sit cross-legged. He placed the back of his wrists on his charred lap, pressing his talons together.

"You've intruded long enough, little Avan." King Waqar formed a bolt on each palm. It sizzled and cracked as it enlarged. Though he tried using his magic before, only to backfire, he was ready to use the bolt to pierce through the young Avan, regardless of the consequence. He caught sight of Prince Mabon approaching from the far right, his wings tucked back and armor glistening. A trio of royals were at his disposal to maim. Only one was needed for the Garghons to triumph, regardless of what transpired outside. He let his bolts die and stood.

"It seems I have all of you in attendance," he said mockingly.

Tori had made a new home on Ava. Not because she was the wife of a prince, but because she loved Mabon and couldn't imagine living without him or her twin sons. But as the years passed, so did the security of moving here. The Garghons weren't supposed to attack Ava, take her babies, or hurt all the Avans she had learned to call friends. On top of that, Xander and Xio were going to celebrate their tenth birthday under the bright moon before puberty hit. On Ava, that meant wings and an uncanny disposition to staying young. There wouldn't be birthdays every year or the kind of family gatherings so common back on Earth. Like Sada, they completed a cycle once every two years, which made Mabon twice what he should be and would allow her sons the ability to stay on with their father. No human could live past what Oda accomplished, yet her sons would be able to, depending on the next two years' development since they were now ten.

Avan physiology was such that if they wanted, they could mate with humans. Only Queen Kalani and Mabon have done so. It was too soon to know whether Sada would follow. Gabriel had confided in Sada's reluctance in the relationship, which Tori couldn't blame. It's scary knowing you'll be the only one dying naturally. Why was she thinking this? She wanted a simple life. Not one where all she could do from falling apart was to work. Though it was odd that only the royals got involved with humans...

"Romeo has returned, my lady," Willa said as she let the dog in. Her face smudged with the day's preparations.

Romeo maneuvered his way past the storage chests she and other Avans were collecting to store food. He stopped at the foot where Urmi sat, making rope. Her dark hair fell at the sides of her cheeks. She was the age her sons were when they first came to Ava. At the moment, she had no wings or an extended life. So young, yet so mature. Then, again, girls always matured before boys, and it was more so for Ava.

The stores of food piled at the corner were neatly stacked by some volunteers. It wasn't right for them to hide in their own haven. *Would Ava ever be safe again?*

"My lady? Are you well?" Willa approached Tori. Her braided hair came loose, and she adjusted the ribbon into a ponytail.

Massaging Romeo's ears, Tori glanced at the tall Avan and asked. "I was wondering who was in charge of deciding who would mate with whom?"

The queen's maid lowered her long arms, bit her bottom lip, and said, "It is for Fate to decide."

"And who is Fate?"

Romeo made a grumbling sound as Tori stood.

Willa nervously looked around. "No one is sure."

Urmi let the rope fall to the ground. "Maybe we should not be talking of this." She pursed her lips, making her appear doll-like with those big green eyes. "A war is on."

"Fate lets the council know, and then the couple." Willa cocked her head to the right and placed her hands in front of her belly, interlocking the fingers. Her right thumb massaged her left. "Some say it was She who made the queen follow her heart."

Tracing the contours of the storage chest, Tori stopped at the Avan symbol centered on the crest of an elaborate bird carving. She couldn't recall the type of bird. "Has *She* ever been wrong?"

Willa shook her head. "Never, my lady, but," her voice lowered to a whisper, "why are you asking me these questions? I am a servant of the court and know little about magic."

"I don't mean to make you uncomfortable, Willa or avoid what's going on outside our doors, Urmi. I'm trying to understand why the royals have fallen for humans." Tori leaned against the chest. "Not that I'm complaining."

Willa bit her lip again and lowered her eyes, then looked up, fixing her gaze at the window behind Tori, where she could see the Avans gathering together to protect themselves in case the Garghons attacked again. "I don't know."

"What if Fate is trying to change the order of things?"

"I don't follow?"

"My children aren't full-blooded Avans, yet they hold power like the royals. Could She be trying to balance something unstable?"

"Having a mate isn't breaking anything, Princess Tori," Urmi said.

The child was definitely Camille's daughter, and Tori wondered just how much she knew about her world at four years old.

Willa continued in an unsteady tone. "Your children might not be full-blooded, but their spirit is, and Avans are the spirit the moon has given."

Tori scratched her head. "Now, *I* don't follow."

Yet, Tori knew Fate didn't just have the royals mate with humans; she or he must have something to do with the Garghons and the moon. Maybe pleading to Fate will end this war with Garghons. If only Tori could get to Mabon and tell him. Wait! Tori jumped off the chest and turned toward the exit.

"Where's Camille?"

"She is forming a spell to aid in Ava's defense out at the edge of the waterfall." Willa followed the princess.

"Mother would not like it if you asked her what I think you're going to ask." Urmi made a tsk. She blew on the loose hair over her forehead, touching the tip of her nose.

"And what am I going to ask that's so unpleasant?"

"You want to be where your family is," the child said.

Widening her eyes, Tori stepped back from them and watched Romeo prick his ears up. "I need to be there. I need to tell Prince Mabon about Fate."

"Princess?" Willa couldn't come up with anything to stop her. It was true; her family was fighting the Garghons head-on and she was occupied up here. She understood how a heart could ache for those you loved. Willa approached Tori and said, "Please be safe, my lady, and let Quoba know I await his return."

Tori clasped Willa's elbows since she couldn't reach the Avan's shoulders and nodded. Hopefully, Fate will choose Quoba for her. "Keep order here, Willa. Romeo will keep you company. I'll return." Then she turned to Urmi. "Will your mother bestow this request?"

"Of course." Urmi's lips slid up on one side. "She has a plan."

CHAPTER
33

Hunkering down to avoid a boulder distended from the surface, Edouard held on to Princess Sada's waist. Her skin felt warm and soft on his callused hands. No sooner did he think it, than he removed his hands, grabbed onto the fin of the hoverboard she created from the slab of rock while fleeing the Garghons, and shook his pulsing head. He watched the stench of smoke, fire, and dampness leave his nose and welcomed the sandy shore smell from the outside, except for the hint of sulfur and decay mixed with it, making him wince. He turned away from the volcano and caught sight of the Avans collecting the bodies of the dead. Garghons were gently placed on one side, Avans on the other.

"What happened here?" he asked in grief.

Sada looked down at the teacher and replied, "War."

His eyes watered as he stood; losing his balance, he grabbed the princess' waist again.

Once Sada set the stone down, he stepped off, knees wobbly from his ordeal in the volcano; his wings plucked from various places prevented his ability to fly. Scanning the littered horizon, he noticed Quoba make his way to them.

"Your highness," Quoba said as he saluted. Then he moved aside to let her view the carnage and prisoners. "Baqir fell, and the Garghons put down their weapons. How fare inside?"

Covering her mouth, Sada placed her free hand on Quoba's bruised shoulder. He took her in his arms before her knees gave way. "I'm all right," she said, dizzy from the unpleasant volcanic smell mixed with everything, and she composed herself. "My father is inside with the twin princes; they are in need of my help."

"Look around you, Princess Sada." Quoba pointed to the beach. "We are in need of someone with select magic. Our forces can't deter the number of Garghons we have, and our wounded need aid. The dead need transporting, and..." His voice trailed off. Wiping the dirt from his chin, he bowed and stepped back. "I apologize, your highness. That was out of line."

Lowering her head, Sada sighed. When she raised her head, she turned to Quoba. "No. It is I who should apologize. My place is here. I will do all I can. I'll contact Camille to assist from Ava in order for Galeno to prepare for the arrivals." She placed her spread fingers on her temples. Her bicolored eyes dulled as her eyelashes fluttered for a few seconds. She exhaled and lowered her arms.

"The prince was right." Edouard walked in front of Sada and beheld the piles of weapons beside a huge boulder. "You wouldn't return to aid them, which means he has a plan in place."

Sada nodded and viewed the soldiers. For once, she wanted to know what Xander's plan was, but not even her newfound ability to venture into everyone's head allowed her entry into the twins at will. They seemed to be protected by something— some higher magic.

"Where is the healer?"

Quoba directed her attention to a white tent by the cliffs where waves smashed against it. "He is with the severely wounded." He turned back to her. "With Gabriel."

Her heart stammered, and she creased her brow. She never knew how sweet his name sounded or how much the mere mention of it manifested a tingling in her stomach. Her eyes brightened, and she said, "Is he..."

Quoba scratched the back of his head. "I mean, Gabriel's one of the wounded."

A lump struggled to slide down Sada's throat. She watched the waves strike the back of the cliff. Once she could swallow, she asked, "How bad?" But Quoba's mournful eyes answered, and she ordered, "Take Edouard to the wounded section. My spell won't hold back his pain much longer."

"Ah, is that what it was?" Edouard crossed his bruised arms. A spasm formed on his jaw, and he smoothed his hand over it.

Sada nodded and continued to address Quoba, "Make sure the Garghons are all in one area so I can incubate them in a holding cell." She caught a whiff of something fresh in the air, unlike the beach, hidden amongst the stench, her stomach creasing from it. Was it an omen? *Oh, Oda, what does it mean?* She waved her hands in front of her face, palms backwards, then she brought her other hand to it, squeezing them together. They trembled, and a bluish light appeared. She circled her forearms, and the light condensed into a see-through sphere. "There," she heaved as the strain of forming a holding pen for the Garghons grew larger. She levitated towards the prisoners' location, bent forward, and blew some air out.

"Are you well, princess?" Edouard asked.

Sada nodded. "I'll start with the severely wounded."

Quoba saluted, bringing his fist against his chest. "Yes, your highness."

She noticed the quiver in his voice and she turned back to him. "What is it?"

"It is Jaime. He died saving us."

Again, her heart stammered. "Does Gabriel know?"

Quoba shook his head.

Her eyes softened, and she placed her hand on his shoulder. A soft white light trailed off her fingers around the area, covering the bruise. "I'll tell him."

She walked away, and Quoba massaged his shoulder.

"She does that sometimes," Edouard said. "A little healing here and there. Just look at me." He pointed to his leg. "I can walk, but the damage is pretty bad."

Quoba formed a slight grin. "Come bird, you might be useful."

Sada headed toward the tent. Her heart pounded in her chest like the drumming of a moon song. *What would she tell the man she pushed away?* Her hand trembled after encasing the Garghons in a dome only the Avan soldiers could open with a touch. It trembled because she couldn't face him. He battled for a world he didn't fully understand. As she opened the tent and saw Gabriel on the cot, she gasped. Most of his body was wrapped in bandages, which were blood-drenched in some areas. His chin was filled with the short whiskers she once teased him about.

"Declan?" she whispered.

Declan turned and raised an eyebrow. His gray eyes, clear as the Hambergite gemstone that made him appear blind, met her gaze. His long black hair with silver strands was laced in a ponytail, and blood was smeared on his sleeves and pants, which would match his red wings if he manifested them.

He bowed and moved away from the Avan he attended. "Princess Sada, I'd welcome you in, but the sight isn't that pleasing."

"The war is almost over, Declan... and I need to know if Gabriel will survive."

"Straight to the point, Princess?" He wiped his hands on a cloth attached to his belt.

"There isn't much time for other tactics, Declan. Oda didn't bestow upon you this gift to worry me." She moved alongside the tent, touching a few of the Avans' feet to calm some of the pain. A faint glow remained on them until they heaved a sigh of relief.

"I'm glad you find it so, for our childhood has always been rather strange."

She scoffed at his remark, taking his hand in hers. She had always held an affinity for him and could understand Oda's choices. Declan was tranquil, fought well, and was knowledgeable about herbs and other things that dealt with healing bodies.

"What were you doing fighting when you were needed for the suffering?" She slid her hand away and moved her sword to the back as she leaned to see Gabriel from where she stood.

"I have to do my part, Princess. The injured piled up after Gabriel was ambushed."

"I don't mean to abuse your role." She stopped in front of him, his torn white shirt with the laces undone, and permitted the Avan's tattoo to be seen on his pectoral. "I know you have your orders."

"Orders I will follow for the royals," Declan said.

She stared into his uncanny gray eyes and nodded. "Show me."

He guided her toward Gabriel. "Gabriel is sleeping. His wounds are deep." He placed a compress on the man's forehead. "He is human and has fought a war with beings of greater strength than he. I'm impressed by his stamina, Princess. I fought alongside him when we landed on the island, and Quoba blew the battle horn. I can see the spirit in him still rages."

Sada kneeled by the cot and took Gabriel's hand in hers. She brought it to her cheek and caressed it, feeling the warmth and courage Declan spoke of. "How faint is the spirit?"

"It only recently faded a few seconds before it returned again."

"His brother died in battle." She massaged Gabriel's fingers.

Declan brought his thumb to his chin. "That would make his return difficult."

"I love him, Declan." The words flowed through her, and

she meant them. *How could she have been so callous as to forget them?*

Raising his eyes, he brushed the loose hair back. "Then it's possible."

CHAPTER
34

Xander flew down to greet his father, who had entered the cavern through one of the shafts. Xio continued wielding his power against the Garghon King, keeping him locked in the net. Yet, it seemed the king could break out soon, which would leave their father to deal with while he helped Xio.

Wrapping his arms around his son, Mabon traced the contour of the white wings. He wasn't present for their spurt and took hold of the boy's shoulders, inspecting Xander's face. "Are you well, son?"

Xander nodded and pointed toward Xio. "We've got to stop him from destroying the Garghons."

King Waqar snarled within the net and asked, "What is this you speak of?"

But the net pressed the creature's body flat as Xio tightened the net around him.

Waqar grabbed onto the net, burning his hands. He pulled apart the webbing about a foot before growling and spitting from the pain. The king's anguished screams filled the cavern, and the scent of seared flesh rose up to the ceiling.

"No, son!" Mabon flew up and tried to pull Xio's arm without any luck. An invisible protective aura surrounded his son's body as a coating. It prevented him from being touched. "Son? This would not solve anything."

Xio's eyes were the blackest orbs, and his dark hair waved in all directions as the wind increased inside the volcano. His wings, the color of night, arched back, and the green light on his fists turned a mustard color, increasing the heat in the volcano. His lips quivered as his arms spread open, the sword glowing in a similar manner.

"Father!" Xander yelled. "Move away—"

But it was too late. A zig zag green light zapped Mabon on his chest from Xio's hand, and the other struck King Waqar on his chest from Xio's other hand.

The light pulsed, and Mabon shook for a few seconds before freezing in place. Waqar did the same. Xio held them with the ray. Lines and perspiration formed on his forehead, and his wings were outstretched. Mabon couldn't believe his son struck him. *For what purpose? Was he confused as to who he was? Or was the power too great for him?* The thoughts continued to play in his head as Xio's fists trembled as if trying to pull back a line, ripping him in two.

Darting back up, Xander could only think of one thing to help his father. He rotated his wrists with fingers wide and formed two semicircle energy bolts and directed them toward his brother's hands, enveloping them in the shapes, cutting the mustard-green ray from their father and the Garghon King. Xander was unsure of the shape's intent, but it seemed to do the job, weakening the rays.

Irritated by his twin's interference, Xio grunted. The sound echoed in the chamber, and more rock collapsed down on top of them, crumbling below them in a heap.

But Xander managed to form a twenty-foot shield in mid-air to protect all of them from the rubble. The shield shimmered each time a boulder struck its surface. Breaking down in a cold sweat, Xander's hands felt an intense pressure, and he watched Xio's hands turn red. Xander gritted his teeth and kneeled. He swept his arm to the left, moving his father and the king further away, then removed the shield so the rocks could hit Xio and break his concentration.

His brother was prepared to destroy them all, but deep down, Xander could tell Xio didn't want to. Facing his twin, Xander took notice of Xio's jaw tightening. The rocks fell on top of him, and the boy blinked but did not fall. He closed his wings over his body like an egg and flew higher up the vent.

Mabon placed his hand over his throbbing chest. There was no mark from the ray, only the Eye of Zorea, bright as the sun. Xander had managed to break Xio's spell.

Raising his eyes, King Waqar, now free from the net, flew towards Mabon and pushed him against the wall. The creature held his chin up with his forearm, pressing on Mabon's windpipe.

"You are to blame for this," King Waqar alleged. "Your demon child will destroy all of us!"

Mabon shook his head for lack of using his voice as the Garghon's forearm pressed further on his windpipe and his foul breath of spoiled meat struck his nose. Massive heat grew on his chest, and it pushed King Waqar back.

Mabon fell forward, coughing, and the Eye burned in his chest like a branding iron. "My son is not a demon!" *Could Xio have released the energy?*

"This isn't the time," Xander said, trying hard to keep Xio's hands concealed in the shapes. His forehead filled with perspiration, and his cheeks warmed.

King Waqar bounced back and kicked Mabon.

"Father!" Xander shouted.

Waqar noticed the light on his chest, then he looked down at his talons. They were glowing yellow, like his eyes. "What is the meaning of this?"

But Mabon couldn't stop to make sense of it. The sulfur in the volcano stuffed his nose and ears. His son needed him to help stop Xio.

Mabon pushed King Waqar back and used a levitation spell to send the creature into the rock wall before he flew to his son's side. He took hold of Xander's hand and closed his eyes to feel the boy's powers soar through him. He opened his eyes and raised his free hand. Electricity traveled from his chest to his fingertips, crackling and popping. Mabon released the white ray to Xio, where it hit his son between the eyes.

With hands locked, Xio gasped and remained motionless as the ray remained in place.

Xander pulled out the queen's amulet, which he managed to bring with him. It pulsed in his hand, and he made a fist over it. The surge of power filled the cavern. The ground shook, and the lava tubes in the dormant volcano flowed with chunky, sharp lava on the floor with small tributaries.

A triangle formed between father and sons above all the lava. King Waqar was unsure of what was happening, except, this was the time to terminate the royal Avans before they remembered he still breathed.

CHAPTER
35

To stop Tamesis from helping the Garghon King, the boy prince trapped her under the rocks. She had never seen magic do this. It was an energy coursing around her—warm and shifting to cold, like a pressure building. The only thing apparent was that whoever controlled the boy would control much more than a mere island, and whoever they pleased to keep as slaves. She scratched the surface of the rock as she thought about her pretty mess, Edouard—an Avan who would have become the Garghon they needed or the puppet she longed for. One who breathed life through his veins rather than being born from death. It was an honor to harbor such a specimen. Nafuna failed in her attempts, and Tamesis had no intention of losing hers. She would claim what belonged to her once again.

She curled her talons and sensed the heat fumes seeping in from the outside. Sulfuric and grainy. To her astonishment, a small crack in the wall poured lava, creeping slowly in. She had to act fast to escape the death trap. Picking her strength up, Tamesis chanted an old verse from deep in her throat, causing the rock next to her to shake and crumble slightly. The magic was strong, and the rock kept its place. With only a fraction opened, she chanted the piece in reverse and watched as the rock crumbled further. Sweat formed around her temples and down her spine.

"This will not be my death bed, boy!" she yelled and formed an echo that shattered more of the rock.

Punching her way through, she noticed the royal family locked in a triangle. Rays of magnificent light stemmed from their chests and hands, connecting each member, while the Garghon King kept a safe distance. *Coward*, she thought, and pushed more rock to fit her wings through quickly.

Other parts of the cavern were filled with creeping lava. *This won't end well.* Still, she could assist the king in destroying the royals once and for all in their locked phase, or... She glanced at the tunnel leading to the outside. Something stirred, and the hairs on the back of her neck stood on end. She focused on the sudden shift in the wind and realized something had landed on the island in an unusual way. Coughing from the fumes, she realized all the members inside the volcano were occupied and hadn't taken notice of her escape. She was of no concern to them or the king. So, she set out towards the tunnel. Whoever or whatever it was will be in for a surprise.

Outside the volcano, a bright turquoise oval appeared, and when it faded, Tori stood amidst the remains of Garghon warriors. She gasped and stepped back. Their black-yellow eyes opened and they stared at her while their arms twisted in various positions. The stench of the deceased hit her like a young man's hideous cologne after they poured half a bottle. The odor consumed her mouth and nose. She covered her face and turned away, only to find fellow Avans scattered throughout the beach a few yards further. Their wings bent or burned, and their faces pale as eggshells. Tears streamed down her cheeks, and she took hold of her aching throat. She wanted to find Mabon and tell him about Fate and what it had done, but she didn't know where to start. Had the battle been over?

"So, there is one more human to deal with, eh?"

Tori gasped, twisted around, and found Tamesis cracking her ashen knuckles.

"I heard you from within the crater. You will come in

handy, female." Tamesis lifted her hands and clasped her palms together until dust filled a sphere.

"Oh, no," Tori said as she recalled the orange dust sprinkled on her sons. The same one was used when Nafuna came after them years ago. The dust changed her sons and turned her life upside down. This time, she wasn't going to end up as another Garghon pawn. Tori caressed the dagger tucked in its leather holder on her hip. She backed away and hit the cliff behind her. Cold and hard on her skin, she stiffened.

Letting the sphere rotate on her palm, Tamesis walked toward Tori, and her free hand slapped the dagger down.

Tori jumped up and hit the back of her head. She tried punching the witch, but Tamesis grabbed onto Tori's shirt.

"How about you scream?"

Tori closed her eyes as a shiver went down her spine. The thing's breath was foul and reeked of molten garlic. She felt her legs come off the ground, and she quickly remembered Sada instructing her on how to escape a Garghon hold, but with a rock behind her, she couldn't see how. The only weapon was her voice, if she could swallow and move past the ache in her throat.

"What do you need me for?" Tori mustered the courage to ask. Her voice filled with a trill.

Tamesis pushed the human against the rock. Tori let out a grunt. "Everyone and everything is up for barter."

"Maybe in your world," Tori said as she opened her eyes and caught sight of the thing's soiled teeth, "but we don't play with other people's lives."

"What do you call what that boy of yours is doing? You think he cares about anything?"

"You made him that way." Tori looked into the creature's yellow-orange eyes and saw the unsure wave forming on them. "You don't know what you did, do you?"

"That boy is a monster." Tamesis released Tori's shirt and let her slide down the rock.

Her shoulder blade hit a protruding rock, and the sting traveled to her neck. "You're the monster killing innocents in order to get your way," Tori expressed in a harsh tone, massaging her neck. "Look around you. Don't you see your armed forces?"

Tamesis bellowed a laugh and turned to view the fallen Garghons. A crooked smile followed, and she said, "They are all replaceable." She grabbed Tori's arm and squeezed.

Tori groaned in pain. The creature's grip tightened on her like a wood clamp. "I... I can't believe you hold no regard for what they have done or what they have fought for."

"This conversation is a waste, human. All Garghons are born to fight for the king. Some more so than others. Death holds them together, and death can take them."

"Your loyalty is most becoming."

"It's not loyalty," Tamesis shrieked, "but fear of our culture going extinct."

"So, you find more to turn into Garghons?"

"We can't resurrect a second time, fool!" Tamesis slapped Tori.

Tori's face burned, and blood trailed off her lip.

"Now," she said, pushing Tori against the rock, "it's time to use you to keep that boy of yours in check." She licked her lips and neared Tori's face. "That is, if he recognizes you."

CHAPTER 36

The tent was filled with wounded Avans, including the man Sada loved. She let go of Gabriel's hand and fell into Declan's arms. She wanted to sob and scream because Gabriel could die, but her family was inside the volcano with the Garghon King, fighting a war neither she nor the Avans were prepared for. All she could do was secure the island to avoid any more conflict, tend to the wounded from both parties, and bury the dead. *The dead.* How many fellow Avans were dead? How many humans? How many Garghons?

Caressing the princess' hair, Declan said, "It's a lot for one person to carry everyone's burdens. Your body radiates an energy that makes you feel more."

Raising her face, Sada met Declan's light gray eyes. "I cannot tend to Gabriel and do what I must for the flock... and I can't ask you to be vigilant over one man when there are so many who need your touch."

"If you love this man, then the wounds will heal."

"But he isn't Avan!" Sada let go of Declan. "He is human, and humans die of wounds like these." She closed her eyes, then reopened them. "He's unconscious."

"And his thoughts are with the people he loves." He took her hand and placed it over her heart. "Love has a way of making miracles."

"Yet, there are moments in my childhood filled with the traces of afterthoughts about a mother who went against Avan teaching." Sada lowered her hand and turned to watch Gabriel's labored breathing.

Her greatest burden involved Oda's powers. She must take up the wise Avan's teachings and guide others. She reached for Declan's face. His smooth cheeks and moist lips were welcoming and distant. Strange that Fate hadn't selected Gabriel for her...

The tarp of the tent opened, clipping her thoughts.

"Apologies, my lady." Quoba bowed. "We need to get everyone up to Ava. The smoke from the volcano is growing."

Sada directed her attention to the Avan and nodded. "Get the warriors to assist with the wounded and move everyone together."

"Yes, Princess." Both Quoba and Declan placed their fists over their chests and bowed.

Sada went past them and parted the tent opening, only to catch sight of the blackest smoke fuming out of the volcano's vent. It flattened into a long cloud heading towards the shore. Sand and cliffs darkened with its shadow, and the sun became covered with a thin raspberry film. Most likely, the gas was mixing with the ash.

Making her way toward the volcano, she glanced at the survivors helping the wounded; their distraught faces filled her heart with strife. "Let Ava's might fill me with the strength to save my people." She made a fist, and Oda's energy flowed through her, causing the veins on her forearm to pop and her hand to swell at the palm with a bright, burning fire.

Time was up, and she had to keep the flock safe. If she was to transport them all to Ava, it would take all her strength to create another island off the coast to save the Garghons. As the energy continued to flow through her, she fell to her knees and was momentarily blinded by the energy. She took a deep breath and punched her brightened fist against the sand.

Waves of white sand bounced in front of her like white crested waves, followed by a thunderous boom that sizzled as it formed a tall dome to cover half the island like an umbrella. The back of her neck was wet, and she exhaled. The dome would keep everyone together to send them off to safety. *Damn if she knew she'd survive this.*

The cavern was filled with intense heat, making Mabon's wings uncomfortably damp and ruffling at the tips. The lava flowing below made the humidity grow for some reason, and his muscles ached from keeping his arms extended. He wasn't sure what his son was doing or the reason behind it. The whole atmosphere could be manipulated without their knowledge. Maybe it was all a play in the mind, and nothing around him was real. Then, again, the weight on his chest was not false. The Eye of Zorea pressed like a heavy stone. Years ago, when Tori was going to conceive, he wished his children would grow up strong and proud to be of mixed blood. If Fate had warned him that the mixing would bring about a stronger breed, he would have prepared better for the Garghons.

Squinting from the light the rays sprung, connecting him to his sons, Mabon recalled Xio as being less conversational than Xander. Deep down, he understood Xio's hesitation about being on Ava. Xio wanted a normal life, as *he* had. Though Mabon was forced to go into it, he had no regrets about living on Earth. Hopefully, neither did his two sons.

"Get ready, Father!" Xander's body emanated a white glow. The yellow-blue rays transfixed between them were thicker yet malleable.

Mabon heard his son but couldn't move. He kept his gaze set on Xio, whose skin was black and whose wings were even darker. Faintly, he could see a gray feather, which relieved him by letting him know he wasn't fully a Garghon. *There could be a way to reverse...*

"Father! Break the triangle," Xander urged. "Xio needs all of the energy."

"You already know what's going to happen, then?" His voice echoed in the cavern.

"We share thoughts, Father, and much more."

Mabon squeezed his fists and brought one hand to touch the other. A force pushed his arm back, but he maintained it, moving as if walking through a wind tunnel. His muscles ached and tensed. The rays followed, but it didn't break the triangle; it kept the rays connected in sloppy lines, as if seeing them through water.

Xander pulled on the rays and pushed them back repeatedly. The rays seemed elastic now. *Rubber bands break when frozen,* he thought as he concentrated on breaking the rays.

In the distance, King Waqar overheard Xander's last remark on the twins' connection. If Xio and Xander were linked as such, then he could have two Avans under his command. The problem was that he also carried with him a power so great that it was impossible to penetrate it. *For the moment, of course.* He knew better than to underestimate Queen Kalani's lineage. It wasn't a coincidence she had chosen a human to mate with. Luckily, Garghons had no need to choose mates or become rebellious against the choice. Theirs was a life born from the remains of the dead. Thus, their hearts weren't made for love, only conquest.

Below, Waqar heard a tussle and warranted a glimpse. Tamesis dragged someone onto a floating boulder and saluted the king.

King Waqar flew down and towered over the human. Smirking, he recognized Mabon's mate, Tori, and gestured for the witch to speak.

"I believe I've found a way to make the young boy do as we like." She raised her eyebrows.

Tori crawled back and gulped. Fear ripped through her bones. Her body shivered even though the place was warming up as they spoke. She turned to view her family in some sort of spell and noticed Xio's newly transformed body. She screamed, and the trio turned toward the sound bouncing on the walls.

"Mother!"

The rays coiled and splashed against Xander, and he spun around. Regaining his balance, Xander took the slippery rays in his hands. He couldn't let another lapse interfere. Xio had to understand. This was the only way he could communicate with him. His mother would have to wait, though, and it saddened him that she was caught between the Garghons and this.

Catching sight of his wife, Mabon whispered her name. "Tori?" His heart sank, but he couldn't break the connection abruptly without hurting his sons. There was a purpose for which Xander wanted it done, and he sensed the Eye of Zorea pulsing inside him, beating like a heart, reacting to it.

Tori reached for them, focusing on their saddened eyes. Only Xio didn't stir. She pounded the rock and cried, "What have you done to my son?"

The Garghons laughed with all their bodies, which made Tori shudder.

"Now, you see the problem." Tamesis picked the human up and held her with one hand. "Your job will be to make him stop, come down, and," she said as she moved closer to Tori's face, her eyes dilating, "have him do exactly as we say."

Tori shook her head. "What makes you think he will listen to me?"

The Garghon King knelt beside Tori; his large frame encompassed the rest of the boulder's top. "A mother's love."

Tori raised her eyes toward Xio. His wings were outstretched wide, and his arms followed. What could she say to make him listen? Was he so far gone that not even *she* could bring him down? Would her calling cause a rift between her family?

CHAPTER
37

The cavern seemed to spin like a huge top. Dizzying. Xio's body was so rigid that his wings wouldn't move. If he didn't use the magic taught him to stay afloat, he would fall, but his brother, Xander, was flying. Wings were so bright, almost blinding with these new eyes. It was like being a cat, patrolling the night for a midnight snack or adventure, and getting caught under the beams of a truck's headlights. Something fizzled through the air; he could smell it. Fire. He glanced at his hands. They were pulsing orange fireballs. *Was he supposed to throw them?*

No.

Xio watched Xander pull on the rays in front of him, tugging at his chest and legs. He was captive and of no use in this position. He had to break free. Closing his fists, the fireballs fell down and disintegrated with the stream of lava below. Then he saw her. A woman covered in an aura so sweet. Scared. His throat ached, and his heart stopped. Gasping for air, he convulsed.

The time had come.

Mabon clapped his hands, and a thunderous sound traveled up, severing the rays from his hands and chest. The blow caused him to collapse against the far rock wall. His elbow struck the sharp edge of the protruding rock, making him bleed from the cut. He frowned and raised his eyes. *Did he break too soon?*

Xander gasped alongside Xio, clutching his throat and pulling on his bare shoulder. After a few seconds, he managed to breathe again, though his chest was tight. Looking back at his twin, Xander hoped the spell helped stop the transformation and gave Xio some control over the darkness.

Xio coughed, and phlegm pushed through his teeth. The slimy salt hit the roof of his mouth before he spit it out. Blood rushed down his nose. The sight only made him grin, for he knew the energy he used was having an effect.

"He's remembering!" Xander yelled.

Tori stood and called Xio's name multiple times. She neared the edge of the floating boulder and got on her knees to prevent a fall into the abyss.

Xio choked, and his mouth filled with a green light. As he spoke, his words were deep, hoarse, and scratchy—unlike his real voice. "You shouldn't be here."

"Come down, son."

"This is taking too long, your lordship," Tamesis said as she caught a whiff of Mabon's blood. She glanced in his direction. He staggered up. The fall must have rattled him a bit. "What about the great prince?" She inquired with a smile.

King Waqar turned away from Xio and narrowed his eyes. He wanted the boy, and he wouldn't let the woman or the Avan take him again. Expanding his wings, he groaned and rammed Mabon, knocking the prince against the rock, winding him, and jabbing his shoulder with the impact.

Mabon felt the hot throb intensify as he grunted at the unexpected attack. He placed his hand on the aching shoulder. Waqar's nostrils flared like steam from a kettle, and his size towered.

"You have no idea what you have created, do you?" Mabon asked.

The Garghon King gritted his teeth and grabbed the Avan

prince's pained shoulder, pressing it back with two talons.

Mabon winced and used his other arm to break the hold. "You hate Avans so much that you sacrifice your own lives?"

"You speak nonsense, but this time, there is no audience to make my army question their destiny." He cut a strap off his chest plate and squeezed Mabon's hand until he buckled.

"You must kill to survive." Mabon fell to his knees as the pressure the king exerted grew. "But all you do is scavenge like a vulture."

King Waqar yanked off the rest of Mabon's chest plate and saw the Eye of Zorea marked on his body.

Stunned, Mabon stepped back and covered the Eye with his hand. Instead of inside his soul, the Eye had imprinted itself on his chest like a tattoo. The lines shone, burning into his skin.

The Garghon King raised an eyebrow and curled his lip. "Funny you should mention it, Prince... or should I call you King?"

"Ibis lied, Waqar." Mabon raised his eyes.

Gnarling his lips, King Waqar's teeth stood out, elongating his face like an ancient African mask.

"The real book that cursed the Garghons was hidden." Mabon pressed further. "The book you took was only a fraction of the dark magic Ibis coveted."

"Lies!" The Garghon King raised his fists and shook them. His horns reached the ceiling and scraped more rock off. They came tumbling off his shoulders.

"Look around you, Waqar," Mabon said, pointing to his sons. "They *are* the book, and they could cause damage to your kingdom."

With reddened eyes, King Waqar glanced back at the twins and watched Xander pull on the rays again. "Impossible."

"My son carries a special amulet. He believes the power originates from it, but Queen Kalani knew better. She placed her power inside alongside its content, increasing my son's abilities."

Scratching his chin, the king curled his talons. "Why tell me all this, *King*? You won't live long enough to see the fruit of your son's labors."

Mabon flew closer to Waqar's face. His neck wrenched in pain as his wounds made his flight unsteady. "I tell you because the Garghons have paid a hefty price for protecting their king and his interests. Don't you think it's time to put all the hate behind us?"

Silence.

King Waqar drew a breath and tilted his chin sideways. The Avan king wanted a truce. The Garghons kept their truce until the twin princes were born. The first set of their kind. It should be the last. After all, Xio had part of his blood. The power Xio held. Claiming him would take a special spell...

"Lord and master!" Tamesis broke Waqar's thoughts. She grabbed Tori and flew to the next floating slab, nearest the king. "Look!"

Xio reached for the ancient sword on his back and sliced the rays his brother operated to hold him. The cut severed the bond further, and Xander came crashing down against the top of a ledge. He was close to getting covered by the lava on the crest, which was flowing steadily away.

Tori let out a shrill, making her head pulse. She couldn't reach any of them and was helpless in their world.

Mabon prepared to fly down, but King Waqar took hold of his wings and threw him against the rock.

Tori bit Tamesis' finger, and the witch let go of her but sent Tori gliding down the slab until something invisible and hard stopped her from falling into the hot, cursing lava. She collected herself and saw Xander's outstretched arm and a large ice wall behind her. Relieved, she let out a cold breath. Soon, her fear returned as Xio maneuvered the sword at an angle across his body and flew toward Tamesis and King Waqar, his eyes an expressionless black void.

CHAPTER
38

Xio drew nearer with the magical sword, as if he were possessed by its magic. Projecting a shield and covering a crouched Tamesis between the boy and himself, Waqar noticed the wings still had a few feathers, and Xio's hair covered the small horns on his head.

The boy prince struck the shield, and a loud spark reverberated from it. A small crack made its way from the side of the shield toward the center. Tamesis screeched and watched as the king stepped back, almost knocking her over.

"This is no time to hide, witch," King Waqar said with gritted teeth, struggling to hold the shield taut. "Make the spell go in our favor."

"It's not that simple anymore." She knelt and drew a circle on the hot rock. "The brat brother has made sure to—"

"You won't have me!" Xio struck the shield again, and it cracked further.

As Xio distracted himself with the Garghons, Xander flew to his mother and helped her up from her fall.

Tori took hold of her grown son, whose wings were as sparkly as the queen's. She hugged him, pressing his body to hers, not wanting to lose him again. She passed her fingers through his hair, and tears streamed down her cheeks. "I thought I'd never see you again."

Backing away, Xander wiped his own tears and looked away.

"What is it?" her voice said, losing the short-lived joy of seeing her son.

But Xander couldn't begin to explain what he knew. He could only say the words that meant more than anything: "I love you, mother."

She pulled him close to her. She watched how the lava bubbles below made his wings shimmer in the darkened cavern. She smoothed the tears from his saddened eyes, and his fists closed. She gulped and turned back to where Xio scrupulously kept striking the shield to get to the Garghons.

"Do you think he'll listen?" she asked as the gas fumes rose and made her cough.

Across from Tori and Xander, Mabon collected himself after Waqar's attack. He shook his head and stretched his wings back and forth while rubbing his sore shoulder. The volcano's gas would kill his wife faster than the rest of them because of their genetic make-up. Time was running out. He spotted Xio with the long sword and headed toward his son.

"Stop!" He placed his hand between the blade and the crumbling shield by forming a barrier that glowed red to deflect the sword, leaving an incision in his skin.

Not able to stop the sword in time, Xio sliced through the barrier, stopping short of his father's forearm before lowering it to his side.

Mabon took his arm and winced from the burning sensation, covering the blood leaking out. He raised his panic-stricken eyes and met Xio's black ones. "Son? It's time to forget this place."

Burrowing his eyebrows together, Xio gripped the sword tighter with both hands and tucked his wings back.

"I know what they did to you was wrong," he said, applying pressure to the cut. "We can fix this."

"There is no fixing what he's become," Tamesis shouted

from her knelt position. She crossed the circle she drew earlier on the rock, and it glowed a fierce blue. "Your son will be no more."

The Garghon king let the shield fall, and it finished crumbling in front of his feet, turning to dust. He shut his swollen eyes from the air inside the volcano and straightened his posture.

"No!" Tori ran forward and stopped short of the boulder she was on. "Mabon!"

Looking down at his wife's distraught face, he let go of his bleeding arm and looked back at Xio.

The boy kept his gaze fixed on the Garghons.

"Xio? You're not what they made you," he said.

"I know." Xio turned his sword around and secured it on his back between his dark wings. "I'm better," he said with a confidence riddled with danger.

"What?!" King Waqar grumbled. He grabbed Tamesis' hair and raised her to his eye level. "Why isn't the spell working?"

Her teeth clattered, and her neck stiffened from the pull on her hair. She reached up to hold onto his wrist.

"What does this mean?" Waqar's nostrils flared fire and smoke onto her body.

She blew some of it away and griped, "It's the spell... it isn't complete without the—"

The gurgling lava shot up at various places inside the volcano, rumbling and cracking the rock around them. The poisonous gas was now making the air thick and putting pressure on their chests and thoughts. Tori, especially, had a hard time remaining standing and propped herself against the rock. Xander had to act quickly.

"The spell can't be complete without the book," Xander disclosed. He held out his hand and revealed the queen's amulet. He placed it against his chest and turned to his mother.

She nodded, knowing full well that she had no role in the magic. She was human and unable to wield such power. The only reason Mabon and her sons had the power was because they were part Avan and royals. Royals got the big power. At least her sons did, and she could tell on their faces that the power could easily consume them.

Closing his eyes, Xander sucked in as much air as he could, and the amulet brightened into a purple glow radiating out into a lighter shade.

Tori covered her face from the light as the amulet disappeared into her son's chest the same way Mabon described the Eye of Zorea entering him, pushing and splitting his chest like a pebble does when having dropped onto water, except the glow remained, and Xander's young face pinched a cadaverous form over it until the rays darted toward the Garghons, illuminating their bodies.

Both the king and Tamesis crouched and took hold of their stomachs as a jolting pain distended their insides.

Whatever it was that Xander did, it ate at him. Mabon flew to him, took hold of his son's shoulders from behind, and focused on his son's thoughts.

Help me...

A tear spewed from Mabon's eye, and he sensed the dark energy Xander had taken from Xio to stop the transformation from being complete. He placed his palm on his son's head, and the other stayed on the boy's shoulder. Mabon closed his eyes, and the glow from his own chest pushed through Xander's fragile body, enhancing the light on the Garghons until it amplified beyond the confines of the volcano, enfolding the other Garghons contained together outside after their defeat by the Avans, keeping them in stasis.

Mabon's arm pulsed with a green flame as the cut Xio's sword made weakened him further. His knees buckled, and the glow tapered.

Moments later, Tori ran to her husband, who had collapsed. She took hold of his head, placing it on her lap. She smoothed his fine hair back with the sweat that formed on his forehead like dew. The Eye of Zorea tattoo was centered on his chest, and she noticed he still breathed as his torso expanded. She took Xander's fading hand. Raising her eyes, she blinked repeatedly, for she could see through her son's body. The skeleton underneath and the bones from the wings were like a bad x-ray printout. She looked up at Xio and shouted, "Do something! They're your family."

Xio cocked his head to the side, but the feelings he should have, weren't there. He looked down at his hands and saw the blackened skin covering them like powdered charcoal. He turned them over and wiped them on his pants, but nothing happened. He swooped down to where his mother was. He touched her face and wiped the wetness of her tears.

Her nose scrunched as she shook her pulsing head.

Xio clutched his brother's hand, releasing it from their mother, and a surge of pain shot up his arm all the way to his back muscles. Dropping to his knees, he caught sight of his skin bursting into flames, but Xander wouldn't let go of him. One look at Xander, and Xio knew he couldn't squirm. He ground his teeth and pounded the rocky foundation. There was a black fog over his eyes, and all the muscles in his body tensed until he lost consciousness.

CHAPTER
39

Xander's body had changed into a transparent being in order to release his brother from the Garghon spell. He let go of his brother's hand, for there was too much power to hold, and left him asleep. His mother held his father on her lap, his face and hair damp with sweat, only intensified the electricity flowing through Xander as he contained the lava from approaching any further. The tears had consumed his mother at the sight of another fallen relative, but Xander had no choice. Xio would have been unstable if he hadn't reversed some of the things the Garghons had done to him.

The power was consuming Xander, confusing what he knew. At least this way, Xio would enter a sleep to rest, for neither of them had enough control over the magic to taper it—only subdue. The energy depleted, and his appearance re-turned: wings bright white and skin tanned. It was because of the magic that a clamp-like pressure on his chest took hold of his heart and squeezed, never to let go. Magic is the curse of their status and the healer of it. It was learned, tiring, and second nature. Tiring. He sighed.

"Are you Fate now?" Tori cried out the words. Her throat ached as if she had a dagger piercing it, but she had to know what her sons were turning into.

Xander knew that the image of seeing through his ghostly

body was overwhelming, so he ignored his mother's question. He placed his overlapped hands on his father's forehead. Xander closed his eyes; the pupils moved under the eyelids while his father's chest rose up and down in sync with his own.

"What are you doing?" Tori grabbed Xander's arm but removed it quickly as the heat surrounding it singed her.

"Father is sick." He opened his eyes. "The sword has poisoned him."

Tori covered her mouth, but she couldn't ask what could be done about it since the Garghon King and Tamesis hovered above them. Their wings were flapping in tune.

"What have you done?" The king demanded, and his wings beat like thunder.

Xander stood, lightheaded; he caressed his temple, then said, "You don't have to be born of death anymore."

"He lies, your highness!" Tamesis squawked.

"Your females can give birth again," Xander said. "The curse is lifted."

Roaring, King Waqar plunged down in front of the boy prince. He took notice of the dark circles under the boy's eyes and the radiance of his wings.

But Xander remained unmoved.

"How dare you?" Waqar bellowed.

"That's what my father was trying to tell you," Xander continued.

"Ibis was many things in your Ava, brat." Waqar waved his arm back, scowl deepening, "But this is beyond her."

"Ibis didn't know that opening a spell like this would break the curse either."

"Hmm..." the king curled the talons on his hands and brought one fist under his chin. The shadows stretched on his cheeks and neck. Things had taken a wide turn from his plan to use the boy prince to seize control of Ava. Earth would have been easier, but the people and animals on it would have given pause to the brat, thinking he was more angel than demon.

Now, he had Garghons who could contaminate with offspring mixed by the death in their tissues. Who knew what would become of them if he didn't sterilize them before they found out?

A large trembling filled the volcano, causing the lava bubbles to burst, filling the cavern with a thick sulfuric and salty smell. Gazing at the young Avan's wings, Waqar lowered his fist and curled his lip at the stench. "Return my army, and you may take yours."

"Your highness! Prince Mabon could be ours once and for all." Tamesis suggested.

"And what good is a King without his spirit?" He gave the witch a sideways glance that cut through her. "We shall find a way to stop the Avans and take hold of their power."

Xander bowed. "There are many who would regard your plan as unworthy."

"And too many have suffered from your schemes," Tori added.

Waqar grinned. "Ava can rot in their mistrust. For now," he smacked his lips, "there is much mending to be done on both sides."

"The Garghons are broken," Galeno uttered. He took Urmi's hand, leading her away from the court where the Avans had gathered to pay tribute to the fallen and congratulate the living.

"And you helped when they landed here, Father." Urmi squeezed his hand. "Don't you think it was bad to let them go?"

"The Garghons were given another chance to live."

"Is that bad?" Urmi asked, confused.

Galeno viewed the yard filled with faces of resistance, hope, and need and said, "To live in peace with them would come at a price. A price we might regret." He pointed to the court as

Avans dispersed from the recent news of Queen Kalani's passing; sorrow overwhelmed men, women, and children. The Garghons' defeat at the hands of mere children only signified that
changes were imminent in the kingdom. He looked down at
his daughter, whose dark curls were put up into a bun. "Avans
will survive this, my sweet, and they will overcome the coming
obstacles because we are stronger than ever and because the
kingdom will prosper with our unity."

Urmi's eyes widened.

Galeno pulled his daughter closer and wiggled his nose
with hers. Camille and Sada had gone to heal the prince—no,
King Mabon. A new dawn would commence after his crown-
ing. It had been inevitable since the day he stepped foot on Ava
five years ago. His mixed heritage wasn't completely welcome,
and now he must deal with the process of trusting the enemy.

Turning toward the hallway, the light from the swan
chandeliers still penetrated the chiffon-white walls stained
by flying debris. Debris was placed there from the Garghon
intrusion, which Galeno would never let himself forget. He
put the lives of every Avan in jeopardy.

"Does that mean the Garghons will stop hating?" Urmi
asked, but realizing her father didn't respond, she tugged on
his finger, repeating the question.

Galeno stopped mid-step and knelt in front of her. "Child,"
he cupped her face, "the Garghons have been dealt with at this
time. It could last a day, a year, or more."

"But Princess Tori said Fate had to fix something broken."
Urmi pouted and moved her lips sideways.

"Fate? Fate meddles and doesn't get everything wished for."

"So, there's no balance?"

Shaking his head, Galeno stood and led his daughter toward the open window where the moon's yellow glow bounced
onto Ava. The night breeze cooled his cheeks, and he looked
down at the dark greenery of his home, where restoration was
to begin the next day.

"Father?" Urmi raised her chin.

Smiling, Galeno smoothed Urmi's hair back. "The moon is part of who we are. Balance is what Nature handles. If Fate could fix and choose every single mate, we would surely be a tyrannical race."

"You mean, no one should have that much power?"

He nodded. "That is why we defeat those who want it."

"But—"

"Hush, child." Galeno placed a finger on Urmi's lips. "Your mother approaches, and I don't think she would want us discussing this. There are too many changes underway."

Urmi giggled and turned toward the door. "I know. She always has a plan."

CHAPTER
40

Tori clung to Mabon's hand as he slept. She pressed her cheek on it and smelled the eucalyptus and peppermint used to wash his body. Romeo sat at his feet; ears perked for anything. The poison that had spread from Mabon's forearm to his shoulder was almost gone. Both Camille and Sada had constructed a spell to cleanse it after Xander stopped the swelling. So far, it had held out. If only Tori could say the same about herself.

She had remained on Ava because of her children. Gabriel wanted to stay on Ava since he didn't have a place to go on Earth. He volunteered to become one of their esteemed warriors. Now, he lay in a special chamber to heal his wounds without any knowledge of his brother's death or Sada's renewed love. Tori learned new skills as well, but was this what she wanted?

Queen Kalani was an exceptional woman, and Tori had learned the value of respect from her. All of Ava mourned her death by planting flowers. Oda was gone, too. He was a good friend and guide. So many had fallen. Fate was something no one could answer at the moment, and Aja, the beast, was placed on ice like Ibis.

"Do you require anything else, your highness?"

Shaking her head, Tori replied, "Not at the moment, Willa, but please... please try to limit the 'highness.'"

"Yes, but surely you know you will be Queen of Ava, and must get used to the custom?"

"I understand, Willa. Thank you."

Willa curtsied and turned to leave the room.

Tori tried to put the past few hours in the back of her mind, but landing on Garghon soil could leave a person feeling unsteady, especially after seeing Tamesis and King Waqar take their army to another location before the island sank. The twins didn't give enough time for regrouping, and Sada had made sure to send everyone to Ava at the last minute. It was probably something not many humans witnessed, let alone lived through.

Her sons had changed so drastically that she didn't recognize them. She still had another ten years to see how her children would turn out before she looked way too old for Mabon. Tears filled her eyes, clouding her vision. Did she have it in her to leave? What of her family? *What about her sanity?*

"Father's better now," Xander said as he entered his parents' chambers. He wore a white shirt without buttons, tucked into his black pants to keep it from opening. He used to think Avans dressed like fancy pirates. Now, he was required to, but he'd rather be studying than figure it out completely.

Wiping a tear, Tori extended her hand as he made his way to her. "What do you mean, honey?"

"Our father is healed." Xander nodded and turned back to where Xio stationed himself by the door, dressed the opposite of his brother in a black shirt.

"We don't want to do this, Mother," Xio said.

"Do what?" She sniffed.

Xio crossed his arms and raised an eyebrow. His skin was tanner than usual, almost like a roasted almond, and his eyes were black orbs sinking into an abyss he was pulled from.

"You heard my thoughts?" Tori caressed Romeo's ears. The dog glanced at her for a moment before returning his gaze back to Mabon.

Xio wandered further in. His stealthy walk made Tori swallow the gulp in her throat.

"A life for a life," he said in a somber tone.

"Oh." She squeezed Xander's hand.

What else could she say? The twins spoke in riddles now. Or maybe it was she who still had difficulty *being* Avan.

"We understand. You want a normal life back on Earth." Xander moved to stand beside his brother. His light blue eye almost white. "You feel lost."

Tori set Mabon's hand down and stood. "Ava needs a king, not a doubtful human."

"Yes. Ava awaits a recuperated king, but he will need you as it is unlikely the Garghons will want peace."

She wasn't a queen. She didn't want the duties, and yet, her children had grown into Avans. Xio wanted to return to Earth, too. To a simpler life. Things had changed, though, ever since the Garghon blood inside him stirred the darkness. He couldn't separate from Xander, whose lead role on Ava was almost equal to Sada's. Tori brought her hand to her forehead and rubbed it; her eyelids were puffy and sensitive. She placed some loose hair behind her ear.

"So, the Garghons will still be a problem?"

"It's not what we think, mother," Xander replied. "The debate has started about whether Garghons will get along with Avans."

"Don't think you're leaving us," Xio added.

Her children could see through her. Read the feelings boiling inside, but did she want to be apart from her family just so she could have her *space*?

"That's not what I want." Tori approached her sons. She took their hands and looked at their identical faces. Though Xio liked his hair longer and scruffier than Xander's, they were alike. How could she abandon them when they needed her most?

"No." She found herself saying it in the silence that passed over them. "Sada has yet to manifest her wings again."

Xio fidgeted with his feet and wanted to loosen his hand from hers.

"Listen to me, honey," she continued. "I love you. Nothing will stop me from doing so." She let go and placed her hand on Xio's cheek. His black eyes were deep and penetrating. "I know the Garghons will return to wreak havoc."

"It is the order of things," Xander pronounced.

She nodded and wiped her tears. "Mabon will have his queen, and the two of you will have your mother until the end."

She pulled the two of them to her and kissed the tops of their heads.

"Until the end," she repeated.

Romeo pawed the ground and licked Mabon's hand as he stirred awake. A smile formed on his lips...

...and his heart filled with song
for the honored cries of loved ones
long passed and newly departed
hold on to the hope for a promising future
that the stained line of Sevilla must yet witness

ACKNOWLEDGMENTS

This book wouldn't have been written without the continuous support of family, friends, and readers. Thank you for allowing me into your imagination. I hope you enjoy this second experience.

Thoughtful appreciation is given to the staff at Atmosphere Press for making this journey possible.

ABOUT ATMOSPHERE PRESS

Founded in 2015, Atmosphere Press was built on the principles of Honesty, Transparency, Professionalism, Kindness, and Making Your Book Awesome. As an ethical and author-friendly hybrid press, we stay true to that founding mission today.

If you're a reader, enter our giveaway for a free book here:

SCAN TO ENTER
BOOK GIVEAWAY

If you're a writer, submit your manuscript for consideration here:

SCAN TO SUBMIT
MANUSCRIPT

And always feel free to visit Atmosphere Press and our authors online at atmospherepress.com. See you there soon!

About the Author

Maria A. Arana is a writer, poet, and editor from the Los Angeles area. She has published many poems and short stories in various publications. Formerly a teacher who encouraged a love of reading and writing, she now channels that passion to create magical stories for a wider audience. She lives with her family, three dogs, and one cat (who thinks she's a queen herself).

You can find her on X (formerly Twitter) at @m_a_Arana and https://www.booksbymaarana.com or at Arana Editing Services, where she also blogs.

Milton Keynes UK
Ingram Content Group UK Ltd.
UKHW021824270524
443037UK00011B/280

9 798891 322660